Overcoming Sadness

Overcoming Sadness

Marjy Marj

ISBN: 978-1-962589-23-9

Table of Contents

THE MOOD SHIFT PLAN

Overcoming Sadness

Introduction

An uplifting guide to overcoming sadness. Crafted from the wisdom and advice of everyday people, this empowering book draws on shared human experiences to provide practical and meaningful ways to heal and grow through life's challenges.

Overcoming Sadness encourages you to rediscover joy and meaning while leaving behind the heaviness in your heart.

The pages are filled with uplifting stories and practices that demonstrate the power of gratitude, intention, and connection.

The book serves as a beautiful reminder that even the smallest actions can inspire hope and transformation.

Pulse Check

How are you feeling today? I'm thinking that if you picked up this book, you may be needing some inspiration.

Some days feel heavier than others. You turn on the TV and it's a steady stream; wars, famine, disasters both natural and man-made, break-ins close to home. It's a lot. On those days, I don't always have the capacity for the news, and that's okay.

And then there's social media. Scroll for a minute and you'll find heartbreak - families grieving, homes lost, tragedy everywhere you look.

Our sadness is no surprise. When the world feels this heavy, it's wise to pause, protect your peace, and choose what you let into your heart.

Have you ever wondered how someone else seems to have it all; the relationship, the car, the house, the dream job? And your résumé feels buried at the bottom of the stack with no callbacks?

Maybe you've been laid off and the search is going nowhere. Or it seems like everyone is getting into their first-choice school while you're collecting rejections. It's human to feel that ache. When comparison creeps in, be gentle with yourself and remember: someone else's highlight reel isn't a verdict on your worth or your timeline.

There's a lot in this world that can make us sad. Our own struggles and the pain of others. I've been writing an inspirational Monday blog to lift my spirits and encourage the people I love. I've realized how much it's helped me. I often cry while I write, and that release has been therapeutic. The page has become a place to let feelings move through, and in that movement, I find a little light.

Like anyone, there are days I wish my pain, anxiety, or disappointment would simply disappear. I'd rather skip the sad moments altogether. But over time, I've noticed something quiet and true: these lows have shaped me. I've learned from them.

Because of what I've been through, I'm better able to sit with others in their hard seasons and offer real comfort. My experience hasn't just weighed me down; it's also given me the tools to lift someone else up.

Sadness has a way of teaching us empathy. On heavy days, I'll scroll through my phone and watch little family moments - singing in the car, laughing in the kitchen, tiny snapshots of joy. Those memories remind me that light still lives alongside the hard things.

There will always be circumstances that bring sadness into our lives. I wish I had a magic wand to fix it all, but I don't. What I do know is this: strength often grows as we walk through what we'd rather avoid.

Life isn't perfect for any of us, but even in the imperfect, we can find meaning and a way forward. One morning, with tears streaming down my face, I reached out to my Facebook community and asked for ways to lift my spirits.

In the chapters that follow, I'll share 41 suggestions from that generous tribe. I've tried every single one. Some have worked for me and others were not a fit for my personality.

This little book gathers the examples my community shared, along with a few additional ideas. My hope is that as you read and explore these suggestions, you'll feel encouraged to take gentle, meaningful steps forward. Please remember: these tips are not a substitute for professional care.

If you're experiencing depression or navigating a particularly hard season, seek support from a licensed therapist or counselor alongside these everyday practices.

Shift 1

- Sing

A.B. suggests singing as a way to uplift the spirit and shake off feelings of sadness.

And so I sang…

Singing has had a two-way effect on me. Sometimes it helps to uplift my spirits and other times it makes me feel worse. I realize that the lyrics have a way of impacting our spirit. When I engage in worship music, I tend to cry more. However, it gives me a sense of relief. Some lyrics have also not been great for my mood. Can you imagine singing sad songs when you've just broken up with a significant other? It'll make you sadder right? But then when you sing along to empowering songs, you tend to feel more upbeat.

In my experience singing praise music, positive lyrics, and upbeat music tend to put me in a better mood.

A few years ago, I was terrified about an upcoming surgery. Somehow a song suggested by one of my colleagues made me feel reassured. So I started playing the song in the shower, the car, during walks and even during my MRI, I had the technician play the song for me. Even as I closed my eyes, I could picture the lyrics.

If you are going through a storm right now, I hope the lyrics to "Jireh-You are enough" will carry you through.

Another song that lightens my mood is Pharell Williams' *"Happy"*. The song helps when I'm doing chores or even on a roadtrip.

And tapping into my Ghanaian heritage, I love those Afrobeats tunes. Sometimes I pretend to be a musician. Davido's *"Feel It"* has a way of making one smile.

These songs have worked for me but may not work for you. I'd encourage you to find your song.

Here are 25 happy songs. I hope a few of these make it onto your playlist.

25 Mood-Lift Anthems

1. *Happy - Pharrell Williams*
   How it helps: Upbeat groove + claps cue movement and dopamine.
   Joyful line: "Clap along if you feel like a room without a roof."

2. *September - Earth, Wind & Fire*
   How it helps: Nostalgic joy resets your mood.
   Joyful line: "Say, do you remember..."

3. *Ain't No Mountain High Enough - Marvin Gaye & Tammi Terrell*
How it helps: Creates support and connection.
Joyful line: "Ain't no mountain high enough..."

4. *Stronger (What Doesn't Kill You) - Kelly Clarkson*
How it helps: Declaring strength out loud builds self-efficacy.
Joyful line: "What doesn't kill you makes you stronger..."

5. *Fight Song - Rachel Platten*
How it helps: Turns vulnerability into agency through vocal power.
Joyful line: "This is my fight song..."

6. *Unwritten - Natasha Bedingfield*
How it helps: Reframes the future as possibility; you're the author.
Joyful line: "The rest is still unwritten..."

7. *Shake It Off - Taylor Swift*
How it helps: Release of rumination via rhythmic repetition.
Joyful line: "I shake it off, I shake it off..."

8. *Don't Stop Believin' - Journey*
How it helps: Chorus fortifies perseverance.
Joyful line: "Don't stop believin', hold on to that feelin'..."

9. *Firework - Katy Perry*
How it helps: Big notes encourage full-body expression.
Joyful line: "'Cause baby, you're a firework..."

10. *Lovely Day - Bill Withers*
How it helps: Positive attitude.
Joyful line: "It's gonna be a lovely day."

11. *Ain't No Stoppin' Us Now - McFadden & Whitehead*
How it helps: Momentum anthem.
Joyful line: "We're on the move!"

12. *Get the Party Started - P!nk*
How it helps: Action-oriented lyrics help to put you into "go" mode.
Joyful line: "I'm comin' up, so you better get this party started..."

13. *Waka Waka (This Time for Africa) - Shakira*
How it helps: The group chant energy builds courage and unity.

Joyful line: "Tsamina mina, eh eh… Waka waka, eh eh…"

14. *Vivir Mi Vida - Marc Anthony*
How it helps: Encourages laughter-and-dance.
Joyful line: "Voy a reír, voy a bailar…"

15. *Three Little Birds - Bob Marley*
How it helps: Reassuring mantra lowers anxiety.
Joyful line: "Every little thing is gonna be alright…"

16. *I Smile - Kirk Franklin*
How it helps: Names struggle while choosing joy.
Joyful line: "I smile, even though I hurt, see I smile…"

17. *Jerusalema - Master KG ft. Nomcebo*
How it helps: Danceable lyrics fosters community and movement.
Joyful line: "Jerusalema ikhaya lami…"

18. *Fall - Davido*
How it helps: Helps to ease tension
Joyful line: "Money fall on you…"

19. *Peru - Fireboy DML*
How it helps: Lifts your mood.
Joyful line: "Peru para, Peru Peru para..."

20. *Terminator - King Promise*
How it helps: Instills self-assurance.
Joyful line: "I dey live my life."

21. *See What We've Done - Mr. Eazi & King Promise*
How it helps: Gratitude for progress reframes hardship.
Joyful line: "See what we've done..."

22. *Walking on Sunshine - Katrina & The Waves*
How it helps: Great for singing loud.
Joyful line: "Don't it feel good!"

23. *Here Comes The Sun - The Beatles*
How it helps: Gentle optimism.
Joyful line: "Here comes the sun, and I say, it's all right..."

24. *Roar - Katy Perry*
How it helps: Reclaims voice and agency.
Joyful line: "I got the eye of the tiger..."

25. *Uptown Funk - Mark Ronson ft. Bruno Mars*
How it helps: Encourages prompt movement and social fun.
Joyful line: "Don't believe me, just watch!"

Music is a tool, and we can choose the right one for the job. Some days call for a song that lightens the mood. You can be intentional with your music, too. Think of it as choosing a song for a specific purpose:

- **An Anchor Song:** A song with lyrics that ground you in faith and trust, like "Jireh."
- **An Uplifting Song:** A track with positive, empowering lyrics that make you feel good.
- **A Movement Song:** An upbeat tune that makes you want to dance.

When you choose your song, pair it with a small action. Breathe deeply through the chorus, try smiling for just ten seconds as you sing, or simply sway or march in place. Find a time and place, whether it's your morning commute or while you cook dinner, and let the music do its work.

I encourage you to keep singing, especially through the storms. Be mindful of the words you choose. Pick the lyrics that speak life, hope, and strength into your heart. You have the power to curate your own soundtrack of resilience, one song at a time.

Shift 2

- Cook

S.S. suggests cooking as therapy - a way to channel your energy and creativity while ending up with something delicious to enjoy.

And so I cooked...

The kitchen became my sanctuary. I boiled, fried, and baked my way through the weekends. I did it all. It was therapeutic for me.

I shared this idea with a few friends. "You should try cooking something new," I'd suggest. Some loved the idea, sending me pictures of their own kitchen experiments. Others just smiled politely; for them, cooking was a chore, not a comfort. And that was okay. We all find our way back to ourselves on different paths.

For me, though, the kitchen offered a tangible sense of control when my emotions felt chaotic. I knew I could make a handful of dishes well, but I wanted to make it a whole new experience. So, I bought a cookbook, filled with dishes I'd never dared to try. My next trip to the grocery store was an adventure. Armed with a list that looked completely different from my usual one, I navigated the aisles with a new sense of purpose, searching for strange herbs and specific cheeses.

Back home, I tied on an apron and got to work. I attempted pies with intricate lattice tops that I'd only ever seen in magazines. I stirred pots of simmering Italian sauces, the aroma of garlic and basil filling every corner of the house. The meals were not always the best. I remember one lopsided pie with a slightly burnt crust. And that Italian dish that my family eyed with suspicion, unsure what to make of its unfamiliar look. They laughed at some of my attempts. Well, I knew my creations weren't winning any awards.

But it didn't matter. The joy wasn't just in the final product; it was in the process. It was the satisfying sizzle of onions hitting a hot pan, the feel of kneading dough. It was something different, a welcome distraction that required all my focus. For a few hours, I wasn't thinking about my worries; I was thinking about how much salt to add or whether the dough had risen enough.

I feel a deep sense of gratitude that I was able to have this experience. I know that some years ago, my budget would not have allowed for fancy ingredients or experimental meals that might not turn out perfectly. Being able to afford that freedom, to play with food just for the joy of it, is a blessing I don't take for granted.

This path of healing through cooking might not be accessible to everyone, and that's important to acknowledge. If a tight budget doesn't permit you to cook a variety of meals, the joy of food can still be found in community.

You could volunteer at a local soup kitchen or food pantry. There, you can help with food delivery, serve guests, or even wash dishes in the back. In those shared moments of service, you can connect with others and be part of something bigger than yourself.

I'd love to hear about your cooking or kitchen experience after you try it. Please leave your review of the experience anywhere books are reviewed.

Also, be sure to check the "Overcoming" chapter at the end of the book for 31 easy, at-home recipes.

Happy cooking!

Shift 3

- Rest and Tune Out

C.S. suggests putting your phone down, tuning out the noise, and giving yourself permission to rest.

And so I tuned out during my rest ...

Small Practices with Big Impact

Phone-down power hour
- Put your phone in another room for 60 minutes.
- Set a kitchen timer, not a screen.
- Do one nourishing thing: nap, sip tea, stretch, or sit by a window.

The quiet day pass
- Give yourself permission to take a full day off from "doing."
- Auto-reply: "Resting today. I'll respond tomorrow."
- Keep it simple: comfy clothes, gentle meals, soft music, early bedtime.

Gentle morning start
- Start the day without your phone for the first 30 minutes.
- Try: 5 deep breaths, a glass of water, and one line in a journal: "Today I choose..."

Cozy corner reset
- Create a small nook: blanket, pillow, soft light.
- Keep a "comfort basket": book, tea, hand cream, tissues, favorite snack.

20-minute nap ritual
- Set a 25-minute timer (5 to unwind, 15-20 to doze).
- Eye mask, slow breathing, no guilt - this is maintenance, not laziness.

Nature minute
- Stand outside for 3-5 minutes.
- Notice: one thing you see, hear, smell, feel. Let your shoulders drop.

Digital Sabbath (mini or full)
- Mini: 6 hours without social media.
- Full: 24 hours off the grid. Tell one trusted person how to reach you if needed.

Single-task tea
- Make a cup of tea or cocoa and do nothing else while you drink it.
- Warm hands, slow sips, long exhales; let your nervous system settle.

Sound bath at home
- Play one gentle track (ocean, rain, instrumental).
- Lie down and breathe with the rhythm for the full song.

Permission to pause list
- Write 5 sentences you can tell yourself on hard days:
    - "It's okay to rest."
    - "I'm allowed to log off."
    - "My body decides the pace."
    - "Joy grows in quiet."
    - "I'll try again tomorrow."

Soft screens, softer rules
- If you must use your phone: grayscale mode, Do Not Disturb, and one-app-at-a-time.
- Move tempting apps off your home screen; keep your phone charging outside the bedroom.

Comfort TV, conscious cutoff
- Watch one comforting episode, not a season.
- Set a stop time before you start; end with a stretch and warm drink.

Warm water therapy
- Take a warm shower or bath.
- Let the water hit your upper back and breathe slowly for 2 minutes.

Five-sense reset
- Sight: dim lights or light a candle.
- Sound: soft playlist.
- Smell: citrus or lavender.
- Touch: soft blanket.
- Taste: mint or honey tea.

One-thing tidy
- Choose a 5-minute tidy: make the bed, clear the nightstand, wash the mugs.
- Small order creates big calm.

"Say no" script
- "I'm at capacity today. I'll circle back when I have the energy."
- Practice it once out loud; give yourself the day.

Cloud gaze break
- Lie down and watch the ceiling fan or clouds for 3 minutes.
- Let thoughts float by without grabbing them.

Rest menu for hard days
- Light rest: sit by a window with a blanket.
- Medium rest: nap + warm shower.
- Deep rest: Digital Sabbath + early bedtime.

End-of-day exhale
- Lights low, hand on heart, slow breath
- Whisper: "I did enough. I am enough."

Shift 4

- Cuddle and Listen to Music

T.K. finds comfort in cuddling an emotional support animal and listening to '80s music

And so I cuddled my pillow…

Comfort Through Cuddles and Music

Cuddle therapy, your way
- Cuddle your pillow, a teddy bear, a cozy blanket, or your significant other - whatever feels safe and soothing.
- Try the "weighted hug": hold your pillow or bear firmly against your chest for 60 - 90 seconds. Let your shoulders drop and breathe slowly. This gentle pressure can calm your nervous system.

Emotional support animals
- If you have a pet, sit with them and match your breath to their calm rhythm.
- Slow petting releases tension. Whisper a simple affirmation as you pet:

You can create an 80s comfort mix:
- Build a 15 - 30 minute mini-playlist of 80s songs; think singable choruses and steady beats.
- Use it as a ritual: press play, dim lights, cuddle your pillow or pet, and breathe.
- Sing softly or hum along. Vibrations in your chest and throat can be surprisingly soothing.

Create a cuddle corner
- Keep a dedicated spot with a soft throw, your pillow or plush, and headphones.
- Add one sensory comfort: lavender sachet, peppermint balm, or a warm mug.

The "hug and hum" routine
- Hug: Wrap arms around your pillow or bear, squeeze gently for 10 seconds, release, repeat 3 times.
- Hum: Pick one chorus from your favorite 80s song and hum it twice. Feel the vibration in your chest.

If you don't have a pet
- A weighted blanket can mimic the grounded feeling.
- Consider volunteering at a shelter for short, meaningful cuddle sessions with animals.

Quick comfort on hard days
- Two-minute reset: hold your pillow, close your eyes, hand on heart, one favorite lyric in your mind.
- Five-minute uplift: one 80s track + gentle sway + three deep exhales.
- Ten-minute calm: cuddle + full song + slower breathing + a glass of water.

Make it yours
- Pair cuddles with scents you love (vanilla, citrus) and dim, warm lighting.
- Rotate playlists: 80s comfort, worship and gratitude, or instrumental chill - whatever softens your edges.

Reminder to self:
"Comfort is not a luxury; it's care."

Shift 5

- Help Someone Out

D.N. shares that helping someone and seeing their grateful smile can lift your own spirits and lighten the emotional load.

An Afternoon Encounter

One Sunday afternoon, after lunch, I felt an ache of sadness as I thought about the family that I was missing.

As I was walking to my car from a local restaurant, I saw two boys standing outside.They were maybe nine and twelve. They weren't begging or even looking at anyone. They were just watching the people inside. The younger one leaned his head against his older brother's arm. My heart skipped a beat. They looked quite sad.

My own sadness felt heavy, but their hunger felt immediate. I paused. I could give them a few dollars and walk away, but something stopped me. My own sense of emptiness felt connected to theirs in that moment, and a simple transaction felt hollow.

Taking a slow breath, I walked over and started talking to them. "Hey, the food looks good, doesn't it?"

The older boy just nodded. His eyes were serious, holding the responsibility of a much older man. The younger one looked at me, then back at the window, his focus unbroken.

"Are you guys hungry?" I asked softly.

Another nod, this one smaller.

"How about your family? Are they at home?"

"Yeah," the older boy whispered, his voice raspy. "Mom's at home with our little sister."

An idea came to mind. "Okay. I'd love to get you all a meal. Why don't you come inside with me and pick out whatever you want for everyone? You know what they like best."

The boy's eyes widened, a flicker of disbelief crossing his face. He looked at his brother, then back at me, searching for the catch. I just smiled, hoping it looked genuine.

When we entered the restaurant, I beckoned to the waitress for the menu. "Go ahead, order for everyone. Don't worry about the price."

Hesitantly, the older boy stepped forward. "Can we... Can we get food for our family?"

"Absolutely," I said. "And what else? What about the sides?"

He pointed. "Some ribs, and a burger. My sister loves burgers."

As he placed the order, his voice grew a little stronger, a little more confident. He was no longer a hungry child on the outside looking in; he was a provider, a son taking care of his family. The younger one tugged on his shirt, whispering, and his brother added fries to the order.

While we waited for the food, I didn't ask them any questions about their situation. This wasn't about their story of lack. When the order was ready, the counter was filled with to-go boxes in brown bags.

I paid, and as I handed the bags to the older boy, his serious expression finally broke. A smile appeared. "Thank you," he said, his voice clear and full.

"You're so welcome," I replied. "Enjoy your lunch."

They were full of smiles. The ache in my own chest hadn't vanished, but it had changed. It felt lighter, as if a small window had been opened in a stuffy room. Walking back to my car, I realized that my sadness had been so inwardly focused. By stepping outside of it, even for a few minutes, I had found a different kind of fulfillment. In the simple act of filling someone else's emptiness, I had unintentionally created a little more space for my own joy to grow back. It wasn't a cure, but it was a connection. And sometimes, a connection is the first step toward finding your way back to yourself.

Below, find a few ideas on how we can help each other out.

Everyday Ways to Help Someone Out

Grocery top-up
- Add a few pantry staples (rice, beans, pasta, eggs, milk) to your cart for a neighbor or local pantry.

Ride or errand buddy
- Offer a ride to an appointment or to pick up prescriptions. If you can't drive, offer to make the call or book the ride.

Bill bridge
- Quietly cover a small bill for someone in a tight month.

Childcare swap
- Two hours of kid-watching so a parent can rest, shower, or catch up on life.

Warm meal drop
- Deliver a simple, reheatable meal in disposable containers. Include a note: "No need to return dishes."

Laundry lift
- Pay for a load at a laundromat or share detergent and dryer sheets.

Job-search nudge
- Review a resume, do a practice interview, or send three relevant job leads with a short encouragement.

Tech help
- Set up email, update a phone, or show how to use video calls. Small tech wins reduce big stress.

Listen without fixing
- 15 minutes of "I'm here - tell me more." No advice, just presence.

Gift a quiet hour
- Text: "I'm handling dinner/pickup. Take one hour just for you."

Care kit
- Assemble a small kit: snacks, water, tissues, lip balm, a kind note.

House lighteners
- Take out trash, wash the dishes, or make the bed. Visible order eases mental load.

Micro-fund
- Keep $10-$20 in small bills for spontaneous generosity - tip, bus fare, lunch, or a warm drink.

Community table
- Organize a "bring one, take one" shelf for books, toiletries, or produce in your building or church.

Check-in chain
- Choose three people. Rotate weekly: one text, one call, one voice note. Consistency beats perfection.

Share your skills
- 30-minute help session: tutoring, fixing a leaky tap, proofreading, budgeting basics.

Practice names
- Learn and use names. Being seen is a form of care.

Invitation to belong
- Invite someone to sit with you at lunch, a service, or a walk. Inclusion lifts isolation.

Joy token
- Leave a handwritten note, a flower, or a favorite snack for a co-worker or friend: "Thinking of you."

Resource handoff
- Keep a list of local supports (hotlines, food pantries, clinics) and share it discreetly when needed.

Help with paperwork
- Offer to help fill out forms, set appointments, or translate. Bureaucracy is hard; partnership helps.

"How can I support you today?"
- Ask this exact question. Let them choose the help. Follow through.

Give and stay human
- Offer what you can without expecting a story or gratitude. If they decline, honor their no with kindness.

Look for one simple way to ease someone's day. Offer what you have - time, presence, a meal, a name remembered - and watch how generosity loosens the knot in your own chest. Helping is not a cure, but it is a bridge. And step by step, that bridge can carry you back toward joy.

Shift 6

- Dance

- C.T. combats sadness by dancing, which can be both invigorating and uplifting.

And so I danced...

I was thinking about my dad's glaucoma. My thoughts were a tangled loop of all the things that felt wrong, and I knew I needed to break the cycle. But how?

On a whim, I grabbed my phone, my thumb scrolling past contacts and news alerts. I just needed a different kind of noise. I pulled up a high-energy Afrobeats playlist, the kind that usually makes me want to move. The opening song - *Unavailable* by Davido - filled the room. I stood up, feeling awkward and self-conscious, even with no one watching. I tried to move my feet, to find the rhythm, but my body felt stiff and uncooperative. The joy in the music felt distant. Although I loved afrobeats, it wasn't working for me.

Just as I was about to sink back into the couch, a different idea sparked. What about the music from my high school days?

My fingers typed out a title I hadn't thought of in years: "Who Let the Dogs Out." The moment the iconic barking and beat started, a smile touched my lips. It was ridiculous. It was goofy. And it was exactly what I needed. I started to bounce. I pictured myself as a kid at a school dance and I let go. I wasn't trying to dance well; I was just moving. I even threw my head back and let out - "woof, woof, woof." A genuine laugh escaped my lips. Marjy Marj was in da house.

Feeling a bit lighter, I let the nostalgia guide me. I searched for the ragga and dancehall tracks that were the soundtrack to my teenage years. As the bass vibrated, the pulse seemed to shake the sadness loose from my bones. I remembered the moves - the butterfly, the bogle-and my body followed along without thinking. My arms swung, my hips found their forgotten rhythm, and soon, a light sweat beaded on my forehead. My breath came faster, not from anxiety, but from exertion. I was no longer feeling as lonely. I was a teenager again, full of life and carefree energy, dancing freely.

After a few songs, the sad thoughts finally broke.

My kind of music may not be for you, but I hope you'll try it. The next time you feel that heavy stillness, find a song. It could be a silly throwback, a worship anthem, or a beat that just makes you want to tap your foot. Let yourself be awkward. Let yourself move.

And if you feel you are unable to dance, perhaps you can watch some dance routines. Maybe you can sit and just let the energy move through you.

How Dancing Helps When You're Sad
- Shifts your state fast: Rhythm prompts your body to move, which signals your brain to release endorphins and dopamine. A natural mood lifter.
- Breaks thought spirals: Coordinating steps demands focus, interrupting negative thoughts.
- Regulates your nervous system: Steady beats support paced breathing and grounding.
- Builds agency: Learning even a simple step restores a sense of "I can."
- Sparks connection: Group classes or follow-alongs create community and belonging.
- Reconnects with joy: Music + movement revives positive memories and playfulness.

Dance Styles to Try
- Afrobeats/Afro-fusion: High-energy, rhythmic footwork and hips. This is great for shaking off heaviness.
- Dancehall/Ragga: Confident grooves (e.g., bogle, butterfly) that boost swagger and self-belief.
- Soca: Fast, carnival energy - perfect for cardio and releasing stress through sweat.

- Amapiano: Laid-back but bouncy; smooth footwork that's fun and social.
- Hip-Hop (beginner): Foundations are simple, musical, and empowering.
- Salsa/Bachata: Partner or solo shines; fluid movement and music that lifts mood.
- Contemporary/Modern: Expressive, cathartic; helpful for processing big emotions.
- Worship/Gospel movement: Gentle sways and lifts. This is soothing for anxious days.
- Zumba/Cardio dance: Follow-along variety with built-in community and instant endorphins.
- Line dances (Electric Slide, Jerusalema): Easy repetition; perfect for quick wins and group joy.

Ways to Learn and Engage

- Start with a two-step: Step side-to-side, add a clap or shoulder roll. Build from there.
- 10-minute rule: One song for warm-up, one to move, one to cool down.
- Follow-along videos: Search "beginner tutorial" or "5-minute routine." Mirror the instructor.
- Micro-routine: Pick 4 counts you like and repeat. Consistency beats complexity.
- Nostalgia set: Make a mini-playlist of throwbacks that make you smile (yes, "Who Let the Dogs Out" counts).
- Worship wind-down: End with a praise song.

- Join a class: Try beginner drop-ins or community rec center sessions. Look for "intro," "foundations," or "absolute beginner."
- Buddy bounce: Dance with a friend on video chat; same song, same time, no judgment.
- Can't dance today? Watch: Play a dance routine, breathe with the beat, tap your fingers or toes. Let rhythm move you from the inside out.

Reminder

- No perfect moves needed. Joy comes from movement, not mastery.
- If you can't move around, dance seated: shoulders, arms, head, and breath still count.
- Your playlist is your teacher. Press play, follow the feeling.

Shift 7

- Spend Time with Horses

- N.P. says spending time with horses is calming and therapeutic. Their presence helps her feel at peace.

My honest experience: This did not work for me. I felt anxious around the horses, and when I tried riding, I was terrified of falling. And that's okay. Not every path to joy will fit every body or every nervous system. The point is to keep looking for what meets you where you are.

N.P.'s recommendation:

With years of involvement at HALTER - an organization that improves the lives of children with challenges through equine-assisted services, education, and research, N.P. has seen breakthroughs that begin with simple presence. Her advice: Be with horses. Start on the ground. Let their calm invite yours. For many, that presence is deeply therapeutic and joyful.

Finding Calm with Horses:

Why horses help some people
- Presence over performance: Horses live in the moment. Their steady breathing, soft eyes, and deliberate movements invite us to slow down and match their calm.
- Biofeedback in motion: Horses often mirror our emotional state. When we soften our breath and unclench our shoulders, they tend to relax too; offering instant, nonverbal feedback that can steady the nervous system.
- Connection without words: Grooming, leading, or simply standing near a horse creates a quiet bond that can feel grounding for children and adults alike.

Ways to try equine-assisted calm
- Start from the fence: Observe. Match your breath to the horse's slow rhythm.
- Ground work only: Begin with grooming or walking beside a horse, guided by a professional. No riding needed.
- Micro-goals: One gentle touch, one brush stroke, one step together. Stop while you still feel safe.

- Choose your horse: Some horses are especially calm and people-focused. Ask staff to pair you accordingly.
- Safety signals: Agree on a stop word with your instructor so you can pause at any moment.
- Alternative roles: If proximity feels like too much, you can still help; fold blankets, fill water, or watch sessions to learn the rhythm of the barn from a comfortable distance.

If it's not for you

Trade the barn for other nature-based calm: walking trails, birdwatching, gardening, or sitting by water. Seek parallel therapies with similar benefits: canine-assisted visits, art therapy, music or rhythm-based practices, or mindful movement like tai chi or gentle dance.

Gentle invitation

If horses call to you, explore an introductory session with a certified program. Go slowly, stay honest about your limits, and let licensed staff support you. If they don't, honor that truth. Joy grows where safety, curiosity, and

kindness meet. Your path can be
different and still be right.

Shift 8

- Seek Learning and Guidance

-L.F. finds hope and growth by exploring Mindvalley and connecting with inspiring people and ideas.

As I was walking through Hub City Bookstore, my eyes landed on a book by Mel Robbins with two simple words on the cover: *Let Them*. I bought it, took it home, and read it with curiosity. The core idea was simple. Let them misunderstand me. Let them judge me. Let them go. It wasn't about being cold; it was about reclaiming the energy I was wasting trying to manage everyone else's opinions. That evening, I did something different. I saw a text that would normally send me into a spiral of over-explaining and defending myself. Instead, I typed, "I understand," and put my phone down. I didn't fix it, I didn't fuss. I let them. Ah, it was peaceful!

This newfound space felt good, but it also revealed the work I needed to do on myself.

I also picked up Brianna Wiest's *The Mountain Is You*. This book showed me how I was standing in my own way, how my own unresolved patterns were an obstacle. It wasn't about blaming myself, but about taking gentle responsibility. The next morning, I put on my sneakers and went for a walk as the sun came up. I didn't set a distance or a pace. I just walked in circles around the parking lot, breathing in the cool air, and acknowledged, "This is my mountain to climb, and this is the first step."

A few years ago, I felt the urge to start sharing my life experience in self-help books, but the fear of not being a good enough non-fiction writer was paralyzing. A book that I found helpful during this process was Faith Cade's *Shine Bright Anyway*. Its message was a gentle reminder. It was a call to show up, messy and imperfect, and to let my light shine regardless. Inspired, I pulled out my writing pad. I didn't write a masterpiece. I just scribbled a few lines. It wasn't for anyone else. It was an act of showing up for myself, of choosing imperfect action over inaction. And would you know it? I finished that manuscript.

When I felt a need to connect not just with myself, but with others. I turned to Tabitha Brown's *Feeding the Soul*. Her words felt like a joyful reminder to nourish myself and others with kindness. Her stories were about presence, laughter, and simple, honest-to-goodness love. Ahhhh. Reading it made me want to share that warmth. So, I went into the kitchen, put on some music, and cooked a simple meal - nothing fancy, just a pot of goat soup. The soup tasted so good.

These books didn't magically solve my problems, but they were guides. Each one met me where I was and gave me one small, actionable step to take.

I invite you to try it, too. You don't need a whole library. Start with one book, one idea. Keep a few sticky tabs handy and mark the sentences that make you feel seen.

Then, choose one tiny thing you can do today. Maybe it's setting a boundary, taking a walk, or just scribbling one sentence in a notebook.

Additional Paths to Renewed Joy

Learn in sips, not gulps
- Daily 10-minute learning block: one lesson, one page, or one key idea.
- Apply before you add: try one action from what you learned the same day.

Platforms with purpose
- Explore structured personal growth platforms (e.g., Mindvalley) for guided programs and community.
- Pair courses with a simple habit tracker: date, idea learned, action taken.

Mentors and expanders
- Make a "Top 5" list of people whose lives or work inspire you (authors, speakers, community leaders).
- Engage lightly: follow their newsletters or talks; note one idea that resonates each week.

Wisdom circles
- Join or form a small learning circle (3-5 people). Meet biweekly to discuss one idea and one practice.

Coaching and counseling
- If sadness lingers, consider a therapist, counselor, or certified coach.
- Use a first-session checklist: goals, boundaries, cultural fit, logistics. If it's not a fit, try another.

Spiritual guidance
- Connect with a faith leader or prayer partner if that aligns with your values.
- Try a weekly rhythm: scripture/reading, reflection, and one act of service.

Learning through service
- Volunteer where you can also learn (youth mentorship, career workshops, community gardens).
- Journal one skill learned and one moment of connection after each session.

Library-first mindset
- Use libraries for books, audiobooks, and free classes; request titles through interlibrary loan.
- Create a "Joy Shelf" at home with 3–5 go-to resources.

Anti-overwhelm filter
- For every new resource, ask: Is this kind, actionable, sustainable?
- Unfollow accounts that spike anxiety or comparison.

Reflection makes it stick
- Keep a small "Learning to Joy" journal: Before/After mood, 1 insight, 1 next step.
- Celebrate small progress.

L.M's invitation
- Follow your curiosity to platforms and people that expand you.
- Let inspiration lead to tiny experiments in daily life. Joy grows where learning meets action.

Shift 9

- Bible Verses and Prayer

- N.K. turns to Bible verses and prayer as a source of strength and peace, especially during moments of struggle.

And so we pray...

Lying in the pre-op room, the air felt unnaturally cool against my skin. A familiar knot of anxiety tightened in my chest. It's a feeling I know well - it sends my thoughts racing.

In moments like these, my mind can become a loud, unruly place. The "what ifs" start to multiply, each one more frightening than the last. Closing my eyes against the fluorescent lights, I began a simple, silent practice. My prayer wasn't formal or filled with eloquent words. It was a quiet conversation, a desperate and honest whisper: *God, I'm scared. Please be with me. I beg you...*

Then, I reached for the words that have become my lifeline in anxious times. Isaiah 41:10. I didn't need to open a Bible; the verse is etched into my heart from repetition. I started to repeat it to myself as a promise whispered from my confirmation.

So do not fear, for I am with you...

The words settled over the beeping of the monitor.

...do not be dismayed, for I am your God.

I felt my own hand, which had been clenched into a fist, begin to relax.

I will strengthen you and help you; I will uphold you with my righteous right hand.

I repeated the verse again, and then again. With each repetition, the truth of it sank deeper, pushing back against the anxiety. The fear was still there, lurking at the edges, but it no longer had me in its grip. I was being held by something stronger. When Pastor Ansley came to check on me and squeezed my hand, her touch felt like a physical confirmation of that final line - I was being upheld.

This practice isn't reserved for special moments. Sometimes, the anxiety is worrying about a difficult conversation or an uncertain future. On those days, I might repeat a different line that has brought me comfort, like the simple assurance from the Psalms that "The Lord is my shepherd," or the gentle reminder to "Be still, and know." Often, I just talk to God as I would a friend, telling Him what's on my mind as I wash dishes or drive.

The world is loud and fear can feel overwhelming, but I've found that a single verse or prayer can create a reminder that we are never truly alone in our struggles.

If you find yourself in a moment of fear, big or small, I invite you to try this. You don't need to have all the right words. Just breathe. Find a short verse or even a single word - like "peace," "hope," or "strength"- and repeat it softly to yourself. You might be surprised at how a few quiet words can make all the difference.

Bible Verses for Sadness, Peace, and Joy

- Isaiah 41:10 - God's presence and strength

- Psalm 34:18 - God near to the brokenhearted

- Psalm 23:1-4 - Shepherding care in dark valleys

- Psalm 42:5 - Speaking hope to your soul

- Matthew 11:28-30 - Rest for the weary

- John 14:27 - Christ's peace, not the world's

- Philippians 4:6-7 - Prayer that guards the heart

- Philippians 4:8 - Redirecting thoughts to what is good

- Romans 15:13 - God of hope filling with joy and peace

- 1 Peter 5:7 - Casting anxieties on God

- Nehemiah 8:10 - The joy of the Lord as strength

- Psalm 30:5 - Joy comes in the morning

- Psalm 16:11 - Path of life and fullness of joy

- Isaiah 26:3 - Perfect peace for a steadfast mind

- Lamentations 3:22-23 - New mercies every morning

Prayer turns my scattered thoughts into a conversation with the One who holds me. Scripture turns the volume up on truth and turns the volume down on fear. Together, they center and guide me.

May you find comfort when the next wave of sadness hits. May His word keep your heart safe.

Shift 10

- Crafts

- K.A. suggests doing crafts to feel productive.

Here are some joyful, simple crafts. Most are 15 - 45 minutes, mess-light, and beginner friendly.

Gratitude postcards
- Fold cardstock, add a doodle or washi tape, and write a 3-line note to someone.

Pressed flower bookmarks
- Press leaves/flowers in a book for a week; glue to cardstock and cover with clear tape.

Calm jar
- Fill a jar with water, a little clear glue, and glitter. Shake, watch it settle, breathe.

Yarn-wrapped letters
- Wrap cardboard initials with yarn or twine; add a small paper flower or button.

Collage cards
- Cut images/words from magazines and arrange on blank cards

Painted affirmation stones
- Smooth pebbles + acrylic paint pens. Add one word: "Hope," "Joy," "Breathe."

Tea-tin candles
- Place a tealight in a clean tin; add lavender buds or orange peel around it for scent.

Simple watercolor blobs
- Paint color blobs, let dry, then outline into flowers or birds with a fine pen.

Memory jar
- Decorate a jar; add one small paper note each day with a happy moment.

Fabric scrap bookmarks
- Glue fabric scraps to cardstock; punch a hole and add ribbon.

Air-dry clay trinket dish
- Roll clay, press a leaf for texture, shape over a bowl edge; paint when dry.

Bead-and-elastic bracelets
- Elastic cord + mixed beads. Add one "anchor" bead for a word or initial.

Nature mobiles
- String sticks, leaves, and feathers with twine; hang by a window.

Tape frames
- "Frame" small photos on a wall or journal page with colorful tape borders.

Mini succulent pots
- Paint patterns on tiny terracotta pots.

Paper garlands
- Cut circles or hearts from colorful paper; sew or glue onto string; drape across a shelf.

Lavender sachets
- Fill small fabric squares with dried lavender; glue or stitch the edges.

Photo gratitude zine
- Fold a single sheet of paper into an 8-page mini zine; add 6 photos and captions.

Button art

- Arrange old buttons into a heart or initial on cardstock; glue and frame.

Tips to keep it joyful

- Keep a "joy kit" box: scissors, glue stick, tape, markers, cardstock, washi tape.
- Aim for done, not perfect; set a 20-minute timer.
- Craft with company: a friend on FaceTime or music in the background.
- End with a share: gift it, display it, or snap a photo for a "made this" album.

Shift 11

- Nature Walks

- J.J. finds solace in forest walks; the sound of water, the birds, and the calm of the trees.

EM-E-FA recharges and relaxes with scenic walks.

Why a Scenic Walk Soothes the Soul

Taking a walk in a natural, scenic place is a remarkably effective way to reset your mood. Our brains benefit immensely from time in nature through something called "attention restoration theory." Unlike the hard focus required to navigate city streets or scroll through a phone, the "soft fascination" of nature; like watching clouds move or leaves rustle, helps reduce mental fatigue.

Walking releases feel-good endorphins and helps process stored stress in the body. The sunlight you absorb supports your circadian rhythm for better sleep and boosts serotonin. A nature walk is also a full sensory experience that grounds you in the present moment. The smell of damp earth, the sound of birds, or the sight of a flower offers a welcome break from anxious thoughts. Witnessing something beautiful, like a sunset or a sprawling tree, can also inspire a sense of awe, which helps to shrink our own problems down to a more manageable size and shift our perspective.

Making It Doable and Kind

A restorative walk shouldn't feel like a chore. The key is to make it easy and accessible, no matter your energy level.

- **Find Your Route:** Look for parks with paved loops, botanical gardens, waterfront promenades, or urban greenways. You don't need a remote wilderness trail.
- **Use Time Boxes:** Don't aim for distance. Just commit to a short amount of time. Ten minutes is wonderful. Twenty minutes is a victory.
- **Pace Yourself:** The right speed is a "talkable pace," where you can hold a conversation comfortably. On low-energy days, a slow meander is exactly what you need.
- **What to Bring:** All you truly need are comfortable shoes. On longer walks, a bottle of water, sunscreen, and a small snack are good ideas.

Accessibility and Safety First

Feeling safe and comfortable allows your mind to relax and receive the full benefits of the walk.

- **Choose Accessible Paths:** Look for flat, paved, or well-maintained gravel paths. Benches along the way are a huge plus for taking rest breaks.
- **Plan for Comfort:** Note where there is shade, especially on hot days. Wear layers you can adjust. Always bring water and use sun or bug protection as needed.
- **Mobility Aids:** Don't let a mobility aid stop you. Many parks have wonderful, accessible paths perfect for wheelchairs, scooters, and walkers.
- **Tech Assists:** Use an app like Merlin Bird ID to identify birdsong or Seek by iNaturalist to identify plants, adding a layer of engagement to your walk.

A Menu of Nature Walk Practices

You can deepen your experience with these simple, mindful practices.

- **Sensory Stroll:** As you walk, notice: five things you can see, four things you can hear, three things you can feel, two you can smell, and one you can taste.
- **Gratitude Loop:** On each lap or at each landmark, name one thing you're grateful for.
- **Color Hunt:** Pick a color and try to find ten examples of it around you.

- **Breath-Paced Walk:** Inhale for four steps, then exhale for six steps. Repeat to settle anxiety.
- **Photo Meditation:** Take five photos of tiny details, like bark texture or light on water. The goal is just to notice, not to post.
- **Scripture or Mantra Walk:** Pair your steps with a meaningful phrase, like "Be still" on the inhale, "and know" on the exhale.
- **Buddy Walk:** Walk side-by-side with a friend. You can chat or agree to walk in comfortable silence for a period.
- **Purpose Walk:** Pick a simple theme, like "find three heart-shaped things" or "notice all the different bird calls."
- **Sunrise/Sunset Ritual:** Make a weekly date to watch the sky change, even just for a few minutes.

Accessible Alternatives for Any Day

- **Window Walk:** Sit by a window and track the movement of clouds or trees for ten minutes.
- **Pocket Park Bench:** A short sit on a park bench, combined with deep breathing, absolutely counts.
- **Indoor Green:** Walk through an indoor conservatory, a mall with plants, or a greenhouse.

- **Seated Stroll:** If you're outdoors but seated, trace shapes in the sky or listen for different sounds.

Make It Stick

- **Prep a "Walk Kit":** Keep comfy shoes, a water bottle, and a light jacket by the door so you're always ready to go.
- **Track the Afterglow:** Note one word for how you feel before your walk and one for after. Seeing the positive shift can be very motivating.

Your Invitation to a Scenic Walk

A gentle walk is a gift you can give yourself anytime. It costs nothing but a little time and offers a wealth of calm in return. I invite you to plan one scenic walk for yourself this week.

1. **Choose a location and a time:** Pick an easy, accessible spot and a 20-minute window.
2. **Pack for comfort:** Water and comfortable shoes are all you need.
3. **Set a simple intention:** Decide to try one small practice, like the Sensory Stroll.
4. **Let go of goals:** Your only job is to walk and to notice.

Step outside. Breathe in the air. Let your footsteps and the beauty of the natural world carry you toward a quieter mind and a lighter heart.

Shift 12

- Meditation and Mindfulness

- V.D. encourages meditating which can bring unexpected joy. - B.F emphasizes mindfulness to process and overcome difficult emotions.

How Meditation Helps Mood
- Lowers stress response: Calms the amygdala and reduces cortisol, easing anxiety.
- Increases emotional regulation: Strengthens attention and impulse control.
- Boosts positive affect: Trains the brain to notice pleasant experiences and gratitude.
- Improves sleep quality: Settles the nervous system, supporting deeper rest.
- Builds resilience: Creates space between stimulus and response, so moods feel less overpowering.

Types of Meditation
- Breath Awareness
    - What it is: Focusing attention on the natural breath.
    - Helps with: Anxiety, scattered thoughts.

- Try: Inhale 4, exhale 6 for 3–5 minutes; gently return to breath when you wander.

Mindfulness
- What it is: Observing thoughts, feelings, and sensations without judgment.
- Helps with: Overthinking, reactivity.
- Try: Notice what's present; label softly ("thinking," "hearing," "tightness"), then return to breathing.

Loving-Kindness
- What it is: Cultivating goodwill for yourself and others.
- Helps with: Self-criticism, loneliness, anger.
- Try: Silently repeat: "May I be safe, may I be well." Extend to others.

Body Scan
- What it is: Systematically moving attention through the body.
- Helps with: Tension, poor sleep, pain awareness.
- Try: From toes to head, notice sensations; soften any tight areas on the exhale.

Guided Visualization
- What it is: Imagining calming scenes or successful outcomes.
- Helps with: Stress, low motivation.
- Try: Picture a safe place (beach, forest); engage all five senses for 5 minutes.

Mantra Meditation
- What it is: Repeating a word/phrase to anchor focus.
- Helps with: Restlessness, racing thoughts.
- Try: Choose a simple phrase (e.g., "Here now"); repeat with each breath.

Prayerful/Contemplative Meditation
- What it is: Silent prayer, scripture reflection, or centering prayer.
- Helps with: Fear, uncertainty; fosters peace and meaning.
- Try: Pick a short verse/word; align it with slow breathing.

Walking Meditation
- What it is: Mindful walking, syncing steps and breath.
- Helps with: Low energy, agitation.
- Try: 10 minutes; feel feet touch the ground, count steps per inhale/exhale.

Noting Meditation
- What it is: Briefly labeling experiences (e.g., "planning," "hearing").
- Helps with: Rumination, getting lost in thought.
- Try: Label once, return to breath - no analysis.

Paced Breathing
- What it is: Equal-length inhale, hold, exhale, hold.
- Helps with: Acute stress, performance anxiety.

Progressive Muscle Relaxation
- What it is: Tense and release muscle groups.
- Helps with: Physical anxiety symptoms, insomnia.
- Try: From feet upward; 5-second tense, 7-second release.

Compassion Meditation
- What it is: Breathing in others' struggle, breathing out relief.
- Helps with: Empathy-fatigue, grief.
- Try: Inhale "pain," exhale "ease," starting with yourself, then others.

Getting Started Tips

- Keep it short: 3 - 5 minutes daily; beats 30 minutes once a week.
- Anchor habit: Pair with an existing cue (after coffee, before bed).
- Posture matters less than comfort: Sit, stand, or lie down with a straight, easy spine.
- Expect wandering: Gently return - returning is the practice.
- Track mood: One word before and after to see what helps.
- Mix and match: Different moods may need different methods (e.g., breath for anxiety, loving-kindness for sadness).

Shift 13

- House Chores

- J.A. recommends doing house chores.

J.R. finds cleaning therapeutic and an effective mood booster.

And so I did chores...

After several hours of listening to the news, my thoughts were a mess. I knew from experience that just sitting with this feeling would only make it worse. I needed to move.

I didn't have the energy for a big project, so I started with the laundry. I gathered the clothes from the hamper, the simple act of sorting whites from colors giving my hands a purpose. I wasn't thinking about solving problems; I was just thinking about the clothes.

While the first load tumbled, I decided to listen to a favorite playlist. With the music playing, my eyes landed on the kitchen counter. It was cluttered with mail, cups, and crumbs from previous meals. Without overthinking it, I started to clear one small section. I wiped it down with a citrus-scented cleaner. The kitchen was smelling fresh.

My mind, which had been spinning with worry, was now focused on the task at hand: wiping, rinsing, stacking plates. I wasn't wrestling with big emotions; I was just making my space a little brighter.

When the dryer buzzed, I pulled out the clothes, hugging the clean, warm bundle. The heat on my skin felt wonderful. I carried the basket to my room and sat on the bed, folding each item. The soft feel of a worn t-shirt, the crispness of a pillowcase…The experience grounded me in the present moment. I paired socks, smoothed wrinkles, and created neat little stacks. With each folded piece, I felt like I had accomplished something.

By the time I was done, the house wasn't just cleaner; it felt lighter. My mind, too, felt more spacious. The knot in my chest had loosened, replaced by a quiet sense of accomplishment and calm. I had taken a space that reflected my inner turmoil and transformed it into a place of peace. And in doing so, I had transformed my own state of mind.

Sometimes, the path back to ourselves isn't through grand gestures but through small, tangible acts of order. When you're feeling low and don't know where to start, I invite you to do some chores. Don't think about cleaning the whole house. Just choose one tiny task. Make your bed. Wipe down one counter. Wash one dish. Let's see if a little bit of outer order can bring you a little bit of inner peace.

House Chores and Errands That Calm the Mind

- Make the bed
- Tidy one surface (desk, nightstand, kitchen counter)
- Do one load of laundry (wash, dry, fold, put away)
- Wash and dry a sink of dishes
- Run and empty the dishwasher
- Wipe kitchen counters and stove
- Sweep or vacuum one room
- Mop a small area (entry, kitchen, bathroom)
- Clean the sink and mirror in one bathroom
- Take out the trash and replace bags
- Sort mail: recycle, file, action pile
- Water plants or trim dead leaves
- Open windows for 5 minutes to air out
- Dust visible surfaces (shelves, frames, lamps)
- Clean the fridge door and handles
- Clear and reset the dining table
- Prepare a simple fruit/veggie tray for the week
- Brew tea or lemon water and tidy while it steeps
- Lightly declutter one drawer
- Fold towels neatly; restock bathroom
- Change bed linens and fluff pillows

- Wipe high-touch spots (doorknobs, switches, remotes)
- Organize a "drop zone" for keys and mail
- Set a 10-minute timer and pick up the floor
- Start a donation bag: add 3 items
- Refresh entryway: shake mats, line up shoes
- Clean a window to let in more light
- Arrange a small bouquet (store-bought or garden clipping)
- Wipe kitchen sink and run a fresh-smelling disposal rinse
- Tidy the car interior (trash, quick wipe, organize console)
- Return library books or pick up holds
- Grocery run for basics (milk, eggs, greens, fruit)
- Pharmacy pickup (meds, vitamins) and restock a small caddy
- Mail a card or package to someone you love
- Walk a simple errand route (post office, corner store)

How these help
- Clear start/finish boosts momentum and agency
- Repetitive motions soothe the nervous system
- Visible progress lifts mood quickly
- Sensory refresh (light, scent, order) signals "safe and settled"

Make it easy

- Use a 10-15 minute timer
- Pair with a calming playlist or podcast
- Choose one "win" per room
- End with a small reward (watch a show, eat ice cream...)

Shift 14

- Teach or Learn a Skill

Have you ever noticed how a heavy mood can feel a little lighter when your hands are busy? There's a quiet magic that happens when you're completely absorbed in a task. For a few minutes, the weight of your worries seems to lift. This chapter is about harnessing that magic by teaching or learning something new. It's not about mastering a skill to impress anyone or adding another item to your to-do list. Instead, it's about giving yourself the gift of an engaged mind and finding a small, steady source of fulfillment.

When we learn or teach a new skill, we invite a state of "flow" into our lives. It's a powerful antidote to rumination and anxiety. Each tiny step forward sends a powerful message to our brain: "I can do this." This builds self-efficacy, a quiet confidence that we can handle challenges. Over time, these small acts of learning or teaching can weave themselves into a larger sense of purpose and even open doors to new social connections.

I know what you might be thinking. "But I don't have time." "What if I'm terrible at it?" "I don't have the right tools." Let's gently set those fears aside. This isn't about becoming an expert overnight. It's about finding 20 minutes in your day for a practice that is just for you. And being "bad" at something new is not a failure; it's a necessary part of the learning process. It means you are trying, you are growing, and you are brave.

In the pages that follow, we'll explore how to choose a skill that genuinely sparks your curiosity, break it down into achievable milestones, and create a simple practice ritual that feels restorative, not demanding. We will look at ways to track your progress and, most importantly, how to celebrate your small, consistent wins along the way. Your journey doesn't have to be perfect, but it can be yours.

Ways to Teach a Skill

- Demonstrate, then do - Show one clear example, then have the learner copy immediately.
- Chunk into micro-steps - Break the skill into 3 to 5 tiny actions; name each step out loud.
- Think-aloud - Narrate your decision-making so learners hear the "why," not just the "what."
- Set a single session goal - "By the end, you'll be able to do X once."
- Immediate wins - Begin with a mini-project they can finish in 10 to 20 minutes to build confidence.

- Retrieval checks - Ask them to explain or teach back one step in their own words.
- Error-friendly environment - Normalize "first drafts"; celebrate useful mistakes.
- Close with reflection - "What worked? What will you try differently next time?"

Ways to Learn New Skills

- Tiny starts - 20-minute sessions; one sub-skill at a time.
- Deliberate practice - Identify one weakness and design a drill for it.
- Spaced repetition - Revisit material on a schedule (Day 1, 3, 7, 14) to lock it in.
- Retrieval over re-reading - Test yourself from memory; then check notes.
- Feedback loops - Seek specific, timely feedback from a peer, mentor, or community.
- Record and review - Short videos or snapshots to spot patterns and track progress.
- Environment setup - Keep tools visible and ready.
- Habit cues - Pair with an existing routine.
- Social learning - Join a class, forum, or accountability buddy; teach what you just learned.
- Mini-projects - Create something small weekly to apply skills and stay motivated.

Shift 15

- Play

- Play in order to channel energy and improve your mood.

My days are usually a cycle of responsibilities. Sometimes a quiet flatness settles over me. I realized that a playful attitude helped me to overcome the flatness. When I came across *The Playful Life* by Dr. Julie Jones and Jed Dearybury, the title felt like a breath of fresh air. As I read, a light bulb went on. The book wasn't just suggesting a hobby; it was making a powerful case, backed by science and soul, that adults *need* to play. It explained that play isn't a frivolous waste of time but a vital nutrient for our minds, relationships, and well-being. It was the permission slip I didn't know I needed.

I decided to take their advice seriously, to intentionally schedule play into my life. My first experiment felt a little awkward. I tried a simple video game that everyone said was beginner-friendly. That evening, controller in hand, I felt a wave of self-consciousness. I was clumsy, my character couldn't follow the steps or moves. For a moment, I felt the familiar frustration of not being good at something immediately. Then, I remembered the book's message: play is about the process, not the performance. I took a breath and let myself be a beginner. Soon, I was laughing at my own silly mistakes. I was enjoying the simple, unadulterated fun of trying.

Buoyed by this small success, I convinced my husband a few days later. "Board game night?" I asked, feeling a little vulnerable. That Friday, we sat at the dining table playing Monopoly. As we clattered dice and moved our little tokens around the board, something magical happened. The structured nature of the game eased the pressure of conversation. We weren't just catching up; we were sharing an experience. Our talk became lighter, more open. We laughed at bad rolls and celebrated small victories. The connection felt easier, warm, and fuzzy.

My playful experiment soon spilled outdoors. During Easter, we brought out a thick rope. "Tug-of-war!" The old me would have politely declined, worried about not being strong enough. But the new, playful me jumped in. I dug my feet into the soft grass, gripped the coarse rope, and pulled with all my might alongside my family. We were a mess of grunting, laughing, and slipping. My team lost spectacularly, tumbling into a heap on the lawn. Lying there, breathless and grinning, I felt a surge of pure, uncomplicated joy.

The most surprising moment came on a random weekend. I was cleaning when I saw a forgotten piece of chalk. On an impulse, I went outside and drew a hopscotch grid. The chalk left a dusty residue on my fingers. After a moment's hesitation, I tossed a small stone, and I hopped through the squares, a bit wobbly and entirely out of practice. A few people walking by smiled. I smiled back, feeling not a bit of embarrassment, only a sense of lightness. I was playing, right there in the middle of a perfectly ordinary day.

These moments didn't solve all my problems, but they changed my perspective. They were injections of light and connection that broke up the monotony. Play reminded me that life could be curious and spontaneous. It re-taught me how to be present, to laugh at myself, and to find delight in the small stuff.

I invite you to try it. You don't need to organize a huge event. Just choose one tiny, playful act this week. Draw with chalk, try a silly dance in your kitchen, or play a simple card game. See how it feels in your body. Notice if it leaves you feeling just a little bit lighter, a little more connected, a little more alive. You might just rediscover a part of yourself you've been missing.

Here are some low-cost, low-prep, and adaptable playful ideas for solo or social moments.

Everyday, Low-Prep Play
- Kitchen dance break: one song, full-body silly.
- Chalk hopscotch or sidewalk doodles.
- 10-minute LEGO/free-build with anything (blocks, cards, magnets).
- Paper airplane contest (solo distance or trick shots).
- Doodle roulette: draw with your non-dominant hand for 2 minutes.
- Play with shadows on a wall or sidewalk.
- Pillow fort + flashlight reading.

Social and Connection Play
- Board/card game night (cozy co-ops like Forbidden Island, classics like Uno).
- Charades or Pictionary with a homemade prompt list.
- Progressive story: each person adds one sentence.
- Tug-of-war or relay races at a park.
- Photo booth silliness: set a timer and props from around the house.

Movement and Outdoor Play
- Frisbee or catch.

- Hula-hoop, jump rope, or hopscotch laps.
- Nature obstacle course using logs, lines, and landmarks.
- Kite flying on a breezy day.
- Soccer, basketball, or tennis
- Sidewalk "maze" drawn in chalk to walk or scooter.

Creative Play

- Five-minute scribble → turn it into a creature.
- Collage from magazines or packaging.
- DIY photo challenges: "reflections," "tiny worlds," "patterns."
- Playdough/air-dry clay mini sculptures.
- Sticker or washi-tape scenes in a notebook.

Brainy and Curious Play

- Riddle hour or puzzle page swap.
- Build a Rube Goldberg machine from household items.
- Speed Lego/brick challenge: build "joy" in 3 minutes.
- Science play: vinegar + baking soda rockets, or floating paper clips.

Digital Play

- Beginner-friendly video games with cozy vibes (creative modes, puzzle/relax).

- Dance or rhythm game for a song or two.
- Co-op couch games for laughter.

Solo Recharge Play

- Coloring pages or paint-by-numbers while listening to a feel-good playlist.
- Pretend "studio hour": 30 minutes to make anything without a goal.
- Dress-up remix: create a wild outfit from your closet and do a mini runway.
- Miniature worlds: arrange tiny scenes with figurines/plants.

Community and Service Play

- Sidewalk compliment station: chalk kind notes.
- Free little art gallery: leave tiny art for neighbors to find.
- Costume walk: themed stroll with friends or pets.

Make it stick

- Schedule a weekly play time (20 - 30 minutes).
- Use a Play Jar: write 20 ideas on slips and draw one.
- Keep a tiny "Play Kit": chalk, cards, stickers, a ball, dice.
- Track the afterglow: one word for mood before/after.

Shift 16

- Movement Improvisation

- A.S. highlights the power of engaging in movement improvisation to inspirational music. She suggests reflecting and channeling emotions through movement, accompanied by deep breathing, which may lead to a cathartic release.

Engaging in movement improvisation to inspirational music is a profound way to connect with your body and process emotions. When we move freely, without choreography or expectation, we allow our bodies to speak. Music provides the emotional landscape, while our breath anchors us in the present moment. This combination can calm the nervous system, unlock stored tension, and create a safe container for cathartic release - whether that comes as tears, deep sighs, or unexpected laughter. It's a way to let go of what's holding you, one gentle motion at a time.

A Simple Practice for Emotional Release

This practice is for you alone. It's not a performance; it's a conversation with yourself.

1. **Set Your Space:** Find a private spot where you won't be interrupted for 10-15 minutes. It can

be your living room, bedroom, or even a closed office. Dim the lights if it helps you feel less self-conscious. Notice the feeling of the floor beneath your feet.

2. **Choose Your Soundtrack:** Select one or two songs that match the feeling you want to explore. Don't overthink it.

3. **Start with Breath:** Stand or sit comfortably. Close your eyes and take three deep breaths. Inhale through your nose, feeling your ribs expand, and exhale slowly through your mouth with a soft sigh. With each exhale, imagine you are softening your shoulders and jaw.

4. **Begin to Move:** As the music starts, let your body respond. There are no right or wrong moves. Maybe you start by simply swaying. Maybe you stretch your arms overhead or trace patterns in the air with your hands. Let the music guide you. Follow any impulse to rock, twist, shake, or be still.

5. **Reflect and Close:** When the music ends, stand in stillness for a moment. Place a hand on your heart. Notice any shifts in your body or mood without judgment. Take one final, deep breath before you open your eyes and go about your day.

Variations for Any Energy Level

Your body and energy will be different each day. Honor that.

- **Seated Practice:** Sit in a sturdy chair with your feet flat on the floor. Explore movements with your arms, torso, head, and neck. You can "paint" the air around you or gently rock.
- **Micro-Movements:** If you feel low on energy, lie on your back and start small. Wiggle your fingers and toes. Gently roll your head from side to side. Flex and point your feet.
- **Walking Improvisation:** If you have space, walk to the rhythm of the music. Change your speed, the length of your stride, or the path you take around the room.

Music & Prompts for Your Mood

- **For Grounding & Calm:** Choose slow, ambient, or classical music (like Ludovico Einaudi or a calming piano playlist). *Prompt: Imagine your feet have roots growing into the earth. Let your movements be slow and heavy.*
- **For Uplifting Joy:** Pick an upbeat, rhythmic song that makes you want to smile. *Prompt: Let the music lift you.*
- **For Cathartic Release:** Use powerful, emotional, instrumental tracks (film scores are

great for this). *Prompt: What does this feeling look like as a shape? As a gesture? Don't be afraid to let your body express sadness, frustration, or hope.*

A Note on Emotional Release

As you move, you may feel emotions rising to the surface. Deep breathing is your anchor. If you feel tears coming, let them. Crying is a natural and healthy physical release of stress hormones. You can place a hand on your chest or wrap your arms around yourself to feel supported. If you feel an urge to sigh, yawn, or even laugh, welcome it. It's just your body letting go. If the feeling becomes overwhelming, simply stop, open your eyes, and press your feet firmly into the floor until you feel grounded again. This is your practice, and you are in control. Please be mindful of any physical injuries, and always move within a range that feels safe for you.

This practice is a gift you can give yourself anytime. I invite you to try it today. Choose one song, give yourself just five minutes, and see what your body has to say. You might be surprised by its wisdom.

Shift 17

- Reconnect with an Old Friend

- A.N. advocates calling a friend or someone you haven't spoken to in a long time. Reconnecting with others can redirect attention from sadness.

I've done this…

My thumb hovered over the call button for a few seconds, my heart thumping with a mix of nostalgia and nervousness. What if she didn't remember me? What if it was awkward? I took a deep breath and placed the call

The phone started ringing. Just as I was about to lose my nerve and hang up, a voice answered. "Hello?"

"Hi, is this Bev?" I asked, my own voice sounding strange to me.

"It is. Who's this?"

"Hi, Bev… It's…" I said my name, and the line went silent for a few seconds.

"No way," she finally breathed out, and then a slow laugh bubbled up. "Wow. How are you?"

The tension in my chest instantly dissolved, replaced by a bubbling joy. The years between us seemed to melt away in that one moment of recognition. We started cautiously, covering the basics. I learned that she had a daughter and was beginning her cosmetology journey. I told her about wanting to visit her.

Then, the real magic began. "Do you remember," she started, her voice full of laughter - she shared memories of our childhood.

I burst out laughing. "Yes!" We reminisced about elementary school. We howled with laughter remembering our old neighborhood. The conversation flowed effortlessly, full of overlapping sentences and shared sighs of, "I totally forgot about that!"

For a moment we were just us, two kids sharing secrets. When we finally said our goodbyes, we confirmed my upcoming visit. After I hung up the phone, I noticed that the stress in my shoulders was gone. That simple act of reaching out, had built a bridge back to a joyful part of myself. It was a powerful reminder that our past connections don't have to stay in the past; they can be a source of incredible light in our present.

There is a unique joy in reconnecting with people who knew you when. I invite you to think of someone from your own past - a childhood friend, a favorite cousin, an old teammate. Send them a text. Make that call. You might just find that a simple "remember when" is all it takes to fill your day with unexpected warmth and laughter.

Shift 18

- Community Engagement

- B.N. suggests getting involved in your community to see the good happening around you.

I love being a part of the community. Here are practical ways to engage with communities that reliably spark connection.

Low-Lift, High-Heart Actions
- Attend one local event per month (library talk, market, game night)
- Join a neighborhood walk or park clean-up
- Volunteer a "micro-shift" (1 - 2 hours) at a food pantry or shelter
- Keep a small stash of kindness cards; leave thank-yous for clerks, drivers, teachers
- Start a weekly "hello walk": greet five neighbors by name

Shared Interests = Instant Bridges
- Join a hobby club (book, garden, chess, hiking, pottery)
- Say yes to a community class (dance, language, cooking)

- Create a casual meetup (Saturday sketch club, sunrise coffee, dog-walk group)
- Start or join a timebank/skill swap

Serve Together, Feel Better
- Host a "care kit" assembly night (hygiene kits for shelters, teacher supply bags)
- Adopt-a-spot: commit to tending one small public area monthly
- Meal train participation (deliver one dish per quarter)
- Write letters to seniors, hospitalized kids, or deployed service members

Micro-Moments of Belonging
- Learn and use people's names (barista, neighbor, security)
- Share surplus (garden veggies, baked goods, kids' books) on a community board
- Offer "third place" invites (library table, park bench, café corner)
- Create a mini free library or little art gallery on your block

Arts, Culture, and Play
- Attend community theater, open mics, or high school games

- Organize a board-game night at the library or café
- Start a seasonal tradition (block potluck, costume parade, summer movie)
- Chalk compliments on sidewalks: "You matter," "Thanks for being here"

Faith and Meaning (if aligned)
- Join a service group, small group, or choir
- Participate in service days or visit/call ministries

Digital-to-Local Bridges
- Use neighborhood apps to find events and offer help
- Host a "meet the neighbors" thread; invite a park hang

Make It Easy (so you'll actually do it)
- Pick one anchor: 1 event + 1 act of service each month
- Buddy up: bring a friend to reduce social friction
- Set a 60-minute cap: leave while energy is still good
- Prepare a simple script: "Hi, I'm [Name]. I'm new to this and excited to help."

How this builds joy:

- Purpose: helping others boosts meaning
- Belonging: repeated contact turns faces into friends
- Momentum: small wins encourage future reach-outs
- Identity shift: "I'm someone who shows up"

May you find joy in supporting your community.

Shift 19

- Journal

- T.G. recommends journaling.

There's a certain magic in a blank page. It asks nothing of you. It doesn't judge, interrupt, or offer unsolicited advice. It simply waits, ready to hold whatever you need it to. For years, the idea of journaling felt like a chore to me-another thing on my to-do list. Now, I know that journaling helps me transfer some of my thoughts or frustrations on paper.

It's not about performance; it's a practice of presence. It's a quiet conversation with yourself and a way to build a more compassionate relationship with the person who matters most: you.

What's Happening in Your Brain When You Journal?

When you feel overwhelmed, your brain's emotional center is in high gear, triggering a fight-or-flight stress response. The simple act of writing down your feelings can help put the brakes on this reaction. Naming your emotions-a practice called affect labeling-has been shown to calm the amygdala. When you write "I feel scared and overwhelmed," you engage the more rational, language-oriented parts of your brain. This helps you shift from just *feeling* the emotion to *observing* it.

Journaling also helps with what psychologists call cognitive reappraisal - looking at a situation from a different angle. When you write down your worries, you can see the beginning, middle, and end of a thought. This distance allows you to question your assumptions, reframe negative thoughts, and see solutions you couldn't access before. It's the difference between being lost in a forest and looking at a map of it.

The Life-Changing Benefits of a Simple Practice

Putting pen to paper (or fingers to keyboard) consistently can unlock a surprising number of benefits that ripple through your life.

- **Finding Clarity in the Chaos:** Your mind can feel like a room with a hundred radios playing at once. Journaling helps you turn them down one by one, tuning into the station that matters. It's a way to dump all the mental clutter onto the page so you can identify what's truly bothering you.
- **Regulating Your Emotions:** By writing through an intense feeling, you give it a safe outlet. It externalizes the emotion, reducing its

intensity. You can rage on the page, grieve freely, or express a joy you feel shy about sharing out loud. It teaches you that you can survive your feelings.

- **Building Self-Compassion:** A journal is a space for radical honesty without judgment. You can write about your mistakes, your insecurities, and your "unacceptable" thoughts. I once filled pages with my frustrations about a project I'd failed. Reading it back, I didn't hear a failure; I heard someone who had tried their best and was hurting. It allowed me to offer myself the same kindness I would offer a friend.

- **Solving Problems Creatively:** When you're stuck on a problem, journaling can be your personal think tank. Writing down the issue, the constraints, and any wild ideas that come to mind activates different parts of your brain. You're not just thinking logically; you're also accessing your intuition and creativity.

- **Tracking Patterns and Triggers:** Over time, your journal becomes an invaluable set of personal data. You might notice that your mood consistently dips on Sunday evenings or that you feel most energized after a morning walk. I discovered a pattern where my anxiety spiked after too much caffeine and not enough sleep;

a simple but life-changing insight that only became clear through my daily entries.

- **Cultivating Gratitude and Savoring Joy:** A journal isn't just for hard times. It's also a place to bottle sunshine. Actively writing down three good things that happened, no matter how small, trains your brain to look for the positive. Describing a joyful moment; the taste of a perfect cup of coffee, the sound of a friend's laughter.

Finding Your Journaling Style

There's no one-size-fits-all approach to journaling. The best style is the one you'll actually do. Experiment with these to see what feels right for you.

- **Freewriting (The Brain Dump):** Set a timer for 10-15 minutes and write continuously without stopping or censoring yourself. It's perfect for clearing your head when you feel overwhelmed.
- **Prompt Journaling:** Use a question or a starting phrase to guide your writing. This is ideal when you're staring at a blank page and don't know where to begin.
- **Gratitude Journaling:** At the beginning or end of your day, list 3-5 things you are grateful for. This is a powerful, quick practice for shifting your mindset.

- **Bullet Journaling:** A customizable system using short bullet points, lists, and symbols to track tasks, habits, and reflections. It's great for people who love organization and visual clarity.
- **Morning Pages:** Popularized by Julia Cameron, this involves writing three pages longhand every morning upon waking. It's meant to clear out the mental cobwebs and unlock creativity.
- **Art or Visual Journaling:** If words aren't your thing, use sketches, collages, paint, or photos to express your feelings. It's a wonderful option for visual thinkers.
- **Audio Journaling:** Use a voice memo app on your phone to talk through your thoughts. This is perfect for people who process things verbally or want to journal on the go.

How to Get Started: A Practical Guide

Starting is the hardest part. Let's make it easy.

- **Choose Your Tools:** This can be a beautiful leather-bound book or a 50-cent spiral notebook. A notes app on your phone or a dedicated journaling program. The best tool is the one that's most convenient for you.
- **Find Your Time:** Link your journaling to an existing habit. Maybe it's five minutes while your coffee brews, ten minutes at your desk

before you start work, or a quick reflection before you turn off the light at night.

- **Start Small:** Don't commit to writing a novel every day. Start with just five minutes, or even just one sentence. Consistency is more important than volume.
- **Ensure Privacy:** Knowing your journal is a safe, private space is essential. Keep a physical journal in a drawer or use a password-protected app. This gives you the freedom to be completely honest.

Overcoming Common Journaling Hurdles

- **"I have to be perfect."** Let go of perfection. Your journal is a "shitty first draft" for your thoughts. Embrace the mess. Use sentence fragments. Misspell words. No one is grading this.
- **"I'm scared someone will find it."** This is a valid fear. If a hidden book feels risky, use a password-protected document on your computer or a journaling app with a passcode.
- **"I don't have time."** You have five minutes. Try the "One-Line-A-Day" method or a simple gratitude list. A tiny bit of journaling is infinitely better than none.
- **"I'm too upset to write."** On days when emotions are raw, don't force a narrative. Just

write down single words: *heavy, sad, angry, tight.* Or try an art journal and just scribble with a color that matches your mood.

Simple Frameworks to Guide You

When you're stuck, a simple structure can help.

- **Debrief:**
  - What was the hardest part of today?
  - Where did I feel it in my body?
  - What is one kind thing I can do for myself right now?
- **Reflection:**
  - Things I'm grateful for today.
  - What I learned about myself or the world.
  - 1 thing I want to do differently tomorrow.

Your Invitation

You don't need to wait for the perfect moment or the perfect notebook. Your story is happening right now. I invite you to take just five minutes today. Grab a piece of paper and a pen. Open a new note on your phone. Start with this one simple sentence: "Right now, I am feeling..." See where it takes you.

Let the page hold your story, and watch as it gently helps you find your way back to yourself.

Shift 20

- Travel When Possible

Planning restorative travel starts by naming your why. Are you hoping to reset your nervous system, reconnect with someone you love, or rediscover a part of yourself that's gone quiet? That intention will shape everything; from how long you go to what you do when you arrive.

Set a real budget range before you plan. Think in tiers: $ for hostels or house shares, public transit, and street food; $$ for mid-range inns and casual dining; $$$ for boutique stays and guided experiences. Decide where you'll splurge - sleep, food, or one unforgettable activity. Pick a travel style that aligns with your energy: slow and simple (one town, daily walks), active and outdoors (hikes and water days), culture and cozy (museums and cafés), or family and roots (connection over sightseeing).

Keep your itinerary light. Plan energy, not minutes; alternate higher-output moments (a long hike, a museum marathon) with low-output rituals (reading in a café, a picnic in the park, a quiet spa hour). Book the friction points - transport, your first night's lodging and one anchor activity. Leave white space elsewhere. Each morning, anchor yourself with a gentle ritual: a 20-minute walk, a local coffee, and a three-line journal check-in. Protect your basics; sleep, hydration, protein, and movement.

To stretch your budget, travel off-peak or in shoulder season, use fare alerts with flexible dates, and stay in neighborhoods just outside tourist cores. Pack light to avoid baggage fees. Picnic your way through a city with market fruit, bakery bread, and local cheese. Look for city passes or transit cards when you'll hit multiple attractions, and consider house-sitting or home swaps for lodging.

Short windows can still refresh you. In 24 - 48 hours, try a rule-bound staycation: book a hotel in a new neighborhood, visit a museum, stroll a nearby park, and end with a simple dinner. Or take a "train to nowhere".

When you're choosing destinations, consider what kind of joy you need. For nature and calm, national and state parks, hot springs towns, lake cabins, coastal trails, and desert escapes deliver quiet beauty.

Traveling to see family can be deeply restorative with a few gentle agreements. Set intentions together; perhaps one shared meal, one outing, and one relaxed evening. Boundaries are kindness: book nearby lodging if space is tight or dynamics are tricky. Plan simple shared activities like a farmers' market and cook-together night, a photo-scanning afternoon, a nature walk, or a board-game evening. To protect your energy, build in solo pockets - a morning walk, a café hour, or an early bedtime pass. Bring a small "joy kit" (a favorite game, playlist, or dessert recipe) to spark connection.

Along the way, look for micro-moments that lift mood: watch sunrise or sunset at a scenic spot, take one "spark photo" each day, write a postcard to your future self, enjoy a 30-minute museum audio tour from a bench, or try a "local kindness quest" with an extra compliment or a generous tip. These tiny rituals create a thread of meaning through your trip.

Travel helps when you're sad because it breaks patterns. New environments interrupt unhelpful mental loops. It refreshes your senses with different light, sounds, and scents, pulling you into the present. Planning and navigating restore a felt sense of agency, and shared experiences deepen bonds with others and with yourself. Landscapes, history, and culture widen your perspective and remind you that life is larger than your current worry.

As you plan, keep a simple checklist:
- Clarify your purpose and time box

- Set a budget range and your top splurge
- Protect your daily baseline of sleep, water, movement, and protein
- Establish joy anchors like a sunrise or sunset pause, a café ritual, and one act of kindness With a clear reason, a realistic plan, and room for serendipity, travel can heal.

Shift 21

- Celebrate Friendships

I remember when colleagues showed up at my door with a small container of soup after my surgery. They didn't stay long, but they made me feel the love, and to hear them say, "We were thinking of you." That simple act was a lifeline. It reminded me that I wasn't alone. In our busy lives, especially when we are navigating stress or sadness, it's easy to let friendships coast. We assume our friends know we care. But actively celebrating those bonds is one of the most reliable ways to lift not only our own spirits, but theirs as well. It's an act of shared joy that creates ripples of warmth and light.

Intentionally celebrating friendship does more than just feel good; it has a profound effect on our well-being. When we connect with a friend, our brains release oxytocin, often called the "bonding hormone," which lowers stress and increases feelings of trust and security. These celebrations reinforce our sense of belonging, a fundamental human need that can feel fragile during difficult times. By creating positive memories together, we build a library of joyful moments we can draw upon when things get tough. It also reinforces our identity outside of whatever struggle we are facing. When a friend sees and celebrates us for our humor, kindness, or passion for baking, it reminds us of the whole, multifaceted person we are.

Ways to Celebrate and Bond

Making a friend feel appreciated doesn't always require grand gestures or a lot of money. The most meaningful celebrations are often the most personal.

Everyday Micro-Gestures

These are small, consistent acts that say, "You're on my mind."

- **The "Thinking of You" Text:** Send a specific, non-demanding message. Instead of "How are you?" which can feel like a big question, try: "I just walked past that coffee shop we love and it made me smile. Thinking of you."
- **Share a Memory:** Send an old photo of the two of you with a simple caption: "Remember this day? So much fun." This instantly brings a shared positive memory to life.
- **Voice Memo Cheerleader:** Leave a short, enthusiastic voice note celebrating one of their recent wins, no matter how small. Hearing your genuine excitement in your voice is a powerful boost.

- **The Tiny Drop-Off:** Leave a favorite snack, a good pen, or a single flower on their porch or desk with a note. It's a tangible piece of care.

Shared Experiences

Doing things together creates new layers of connection.

- **Parallel Play Date:** If you're both feeling low-energy, just be in the same space without pressure to talk. Sit in a park and read your own books, or work on separate projects at the same kitchen table.
- **Golden Hour Walk:** Meet up for a walk during that beautiful time just before sunset. The soft light and gentle movement create a perfect container for easy conversation.
- **Co-op Game Night:** Instead of competitive games, choose a cooperative board game or video game where you work together toward a common goal. It's all the fun with none of the rivalry.
- **Learn Something Together:** Sign up for a low-stakes, one-night class; pottery, pasta making, or even a silly dance class. The shared vulnerability of being a beginner is a powerful bonder.

Mark-the-Moment Rituals

These are for celebrating milestones beyond just birthdays.

- **Friendship Anniversary:** Note the day you met or a significant moment in your friendship. Celebrate it each year with a call, a coffee, or a card.
- **"Got-the-Job" or "Survived-the-Week" Toast:** Create a ritual around celebrating wins, both big and small. It can be as simple as a video call toast or meeting at a favorite spot for a special drink.
- **The "Reverse Surprise Party":** For a friend going through a hard time, organize a "care party" where a few close friends show up for an hour to do something helpful. Like folding laundry, cooking a meal, or walking the dog.

Words and Keepsakes

Sometimes, spelling out your appreciation is the most powerful gift.

- **The "Qualities I Admire" List:** Write a simple, bulleted list of things you love and admire about your friend. "Your incredible patience," "The way you laugh with your whole body,"

"Your brilliant mind." It's a deeply meaningful and free gift.

- **Create a Shared Playlist:** Build a collaborative playlist with songs that remind you of your friendship, your inside jokes, or songs you think they'd love.
- **The Friendship Jar:** Fill a jar with small, folded notes containing favorite memories, inside jokes, and words of encouragement. Tell your friend to pull one out whenever they need a lift.

Long-Distance Celebrations

Connection knows no geography.

- **Watch Party:** Use a streaming service feature to watch a movie or a TV show premiere at the same time. Keep a text thread going with your running commentary.
- **Care Package with a Theme:** Send a small box of things based on an inside joke or a shared interest, like a "Cozy Night In" kit with tea, fuzzy socks, and a good book.
- **Snail Mail Surprise:** In a world of instant messages, a handwritten letter stands out. Share what's been on your mind and ask them questions, creating a slow, thoughtful conversation.

A Note on Inclusive Celebration

To make your celebration truly joyful, ensure it works for your friend. Consider their budget and suggest free or low-cost options. Be mindful of their social energy; a big party might be draining for an introverted friend, while a quiet one-on-one would be perfect. Always ask what feels good to them.

Your Invitation to Connect

Celebrating friendship is a practice, a muscle we can strengthen. It's one of the most powerful and accessible tools we have to combat loneliness and bring genuine joy into our lives. This week, I invite you to pick just one person and one small action from this list. Send that text, share that photo, or schedule that walk. Let a friend know they matter. You may find that the warmth you generate for them comes right back to brighten your own day.

Shift 22

- Morning Tranquility

- B.B. enjoys sitting outside in the early morning, observing the beauty of nature.

Exposure to natural light shortly after waking helps to reset our body's internal clock. It signals to our brain to decrease melatonin (the sleep hormone) and provides a gentle, natural spike in cortisol, the hormone that helps us feel alert and engaged. When we start our day with quiet intention instead of digital noise and rushing, we give our nervous system a chance to come online calmly. We set a tone of presence and gentleness that we can carry with us long after the sun is high in the sky.

Crafting a tranquil morning isn't about adding more to your to-do list; it's about curating a few moments of peace before the world demands your attention. You can build a restorative routine that fits your energy level and the time you have.

A Menu of Gentle Morning Practices

- **Greet the Light (2 minutes):** Before you look at a screen, look out a window. Stand there and simply notice the color of the sky. If you can, step outside for just a moment and let the light hit your face.

- **Breath and Stretch (5 minutes):** Sit on the edge of your bed. Take three slow, deep breaths. As you inhale, stretch your arms overhead. As you exhale, let them fall. Gently roll your neck and shoulders. Let your body wake up slowly.
- **Warm Beverage Ritual (5 minutes):** Prepare a cup of tea, coffee, or hot water with lemon. Pay attention to the whole process: the sound of the water, the warmth of the mug in your hands, the first sip. Make it a moment of mindful sensory input.
- **One-Sentence Journal (2 minutes):** In a notebook by your bed, write down just one sentence. It could be an intention for the day or a single observation.
- **The Nature Glance (2 minutes):** Find one natural thing to look at: a houseplant, a tree outside your window, a cloud. Notice its details for sixty seconds. This simple act pulls you into the present.
- **The Tiny Tidy (5 minutes):** Don't clean the whole house. Just do one small thing that will make your space feel better: make your bed, put one dish in the dishwasher, or wipe down the kitchen counter. A small act of order can create a feeling of inner calm.

- **Compassionate Planning (10 minutes):** Instead of a frantic to-do list, look at your day and ask, "What is the one thing that truly matters today?" and "Where can I build in a moment of rest?"

Making It Possible

The key to a tranquil morning is reducing friction. A few small steps the night before can make all the difference.

- **Prep Your Space:** Set out your mug and teabag. Put your journal and pen on your nightstand. Lay out your clothes. Create an inviting path to your peaceful morning.
- **Set Phone Boundaries:** The morning is for you, not your inbox or social media feed. Try keeping your phone in another room or leaving it on airplane mode for the first 30 minutes of your day.
- **Start Small:** Don't try to implement all of these ideas at once. Choose just one. Try it for a week. A two-minute habit practiced consistently is more powerful than a 30-minute routine that you only do once.

Your morning holds an invitation to begin your day with grace. You don't need a perfect sunrise or an hour of free time. All you need is the intention to claim a few quiet moments for yourself. I invite you to try one tiny thing differently tomorrow morning. Open a window, stretch your arms to the sky, or savor a warm drink in silence. Greet the day gently, and let it greet you back.

Shift 23

- Sunshine

- M.C. recommends sitting in the sunshine to find warmth and peace.

Sunshine helps lift mood by resetting your body clock in the morning, which lowers melatonin and increases alertness at the right time. Bright light exposure is linked to increased serotonin activity, supporting calm, focus, and a general sense of well-being. This can counter low mood and seasonal dips. Natural light also supports a healthy cortisol awakening response shortly after you wake, helping you feel motivated without feeling wired.

Being outdoors in bright light reduces mental fatigue and rumination, restoring attention and nudging you into a more present, optimistic state. You can use these benefits by getting five to ten minutes of light outside within an hour of waking, working near a bright window or taking a brief sun break at midday, and pairing sunlight with gentle movement for an extra lift. On darker days, you can open blinds, sit near windows, or use a clinician-recommended light box if appropriate.

As always, protect your skin and eyes with sensible exposure and sunscreen when UV is high, and check with a clinician if you have light-sensitive conditions or take photosensitizing medications.

May you find joy in the sun.

Shift 24

- Crying as Emotional Release

- B.L. encourages allowing oneself to cry, describing it as a powerful emotional and physical reset.

Let's normalize crying...

I spent years believing that crying was a sign of weakness, a failure of control. I'd bite my lip, stare at the ceiling, and swallow the lump in my throat, convinced that holding it all together was the strong thing to do. Now I know that tears are not a breakdown, but a breakthrough. They are the body's natural and incredibly effective way of releasing pressure, processing pain, and beginning the process of healing. Crying is not the moment you fall apart; it's the moment you begin to put yourself back together in a more honest way.

What's Happening When You Cry?

When you allow yourself to have a good cry, you are triggering a cascade of helpful physiological responses. Your tears are doing far more than just rolling down your cheeks. This is your body's built-in reset button.

First, the act of deep crying often involves changes in your breathing; hitching sobs followed by long exhales. This process stimulates the parasympathetic nervous system, our body's "rest and digest" system. It acts as a natural brake on the "fight or flight" stress response, helping to lower your heart rate and bring a sense of calm after the emotional storm has passed.

Emotional tears, the kind that come from sadness, grief, or even overwhelming joy are chemically different from the tears that just lubricate your eyes. They have been found to contain stress hormones and other toxins. Some researchers believe that by crying, you are literally flushing these substances out of your system, lightening your physiological load. Furthermore, crying can trigger the release of oxytocin and endorphins. These are the body's natural "feel-good" chemicals, providing a gentle sense of comfort, well-being, and pain relief. It's why you often feel a sense of quiet exhaustion and relief after a good cry. Your body has just given you a dose of its own soothing balm.

The Right Time for Tears

Crying is a powerful tool, and like any tool, it is most helpful in certain situations. It's a healthy response when you are navigating waves of grief, allowing you to honor your loss and move through the pain rather than getting stuck in it. It's also an incredible release valve for accumulated stress. After a week of holding it together, a cathartic cry can feel like finally putting down a heavy bag you didn't realize you were carrying. It can also bring surprising clarity. When you've been bottling up feelings, they can become a confusing, tangled mess. The release of a cry can sometimes clear the mental fog, helping you understand what you are truly feeling underneath all the noise.

Sharing tears with a trusted friend or partner can also be a profound bonding experience. It signals vulnerability and trust, deepening intimacy and inviting comfort. However, it's also important to check in with yourself. If you find yourself crying constantly, feeling a persistent sense of hopelessness, and it's impairing your ability to function in daily life, it may be a sign that you need more support from a therapist or counselor.

How to Create a Safe Space for Release

Our culture often teaches us to cry in private, if at all. Reclaiming crying as a healthy practice means creating a safe container for it.

1. **Find Your Sanctuary:** Choose a time and place where you won't be interrupted or feel self-conscious. This might be your bedroom, your car, or even a bathroom.

2. **Get Comfortable:** Your posture matters. Instead of hunching over and tensing up, try lying on your side or sitting with your back supported. Place a hand on your heart or belly to offer yourself a physical sense of comfort.
3. **Breathe:** As tears begin to well, focus on your exhale. Let it be long and slow. This signals to your nervous system that you are safe.
4. **Ground Yourself:** Keep a soft blanket, a warm drink, or a smooth stone nearby. The physical sensation can help you feel anchored if the emotions feel overwhelming.
5. **Practice Aftercare:** Crying is an expenditure of energy. Afterward, be gentle with yourself. Drink a glass of water, splash cool water on your face, or lie down for a few minutes. You might also find it helpful to journal about what came up, without judgment.

Gently Inviting Your Tears

Sometimes you can feel the need to cry, but the tears just won't come. You don't have to force it, but you can create an invitation.

- **Music:** Put on a piece of music that you find deeply moving. It could be a powerful film score, a sad song from your past, or a beautiful classical piece.

- **Movement:** Put on that music and gently sway or stretch. Let your body express the feeling that is stuck inside.
- **Writing:** Open a journal and write a letter to the part of you that is hurting. Start with, "Dear Sadness..." or "To the part of me that feels overwhelmed..."
- **Imagery:** Close your eyes and imagine the feeling as a physical object inside you. What does it look like? What would happen if you just gave it a little space to soften or dissolve?

If tears still don't come, that's okay. The act of creating space and listening to your body is healing in itself. Simply sitting with the feeling is a courageous first step.

Your Invitation to Feel

We have been taught that strength is about holding back, but true strength lies in the courage to feel. It's in allowing our natural emotional processes to unfold, trusting that our bodies know how to heal. Crying is a sign that you are engaged, you are processing, and you are alive. I invite you to set aside just five or ten minutes this week. Find a quiet space, put a hand on your heart, and whisper to yourself, "It's safe to feel this now." You don't need to do anything else. Just create a small pocket of permission and see what happens.

Your tears are not your enemy; they are part of your wisdom.

Shift 25

- Expressing Gratitude

- A.H. encourages us to express gratitude.

Why Gratitude Lifts Your Mood

Practicing gratitude is more than just being polite; it's a powerful mental exercise that can rewire your brain for happiness. Our brains are naturally wired with a "negativity bias," meaning we tend to pay more attention to threats and problems. Intentionally looking for things to be grateful for trains your brain to notice the good. It's like adjusting a filter to let more light in. Over time, your brain gets better at automatically spotting positives.

This simple shift has a real biological effect. When you focus on a feeling of gratitude, your brain can release feel-good neurotransmitters like dopamine and serotonin, which help to lift your mood and create a sense of well-being. Gratitude also pulls you out of the loop of your own worries and connects you to the world outside yourself. It fosters a sense of meaning and reminds you of the relationships and resources that support you, which is a powerful antidote to feelings of isolation and stress.

Simple Daily Gratitude Practices

You don't need to make a grand gesture. The most effective gratitude practices are small and consistent.

- **Three Good Things:** At the end of each day, write down three things that went well and why. They can be tiny, like "I enjoyed my morning coffee because it was hot and quiet."
- **Gratitude Breath:** Take a moment to breathe in, and as you exhale, think of one thing you are grateful for right now.
- **Thank-You Text:** Send a quick text or voice note to a friend, simply saying, "Thinking of you and grateful for our friendship."
- **Mealtime Gratitude:** Before you eat, pause for a moment to feel thankful for the food and the people who helped bring it to your table.
- **Bedtime Recap:** As you lie in bed, mentally scan your day and pick out one positive moment to hold in your mind as you drift off to sleep.

Creative Ways to Express Gratitude

If journaling isn't for you, try one of these more active methods.

- **Gratitude Walk:** Go for a walk with the sole intention of noticing things you are grateful for. For example, the feeling of the sun, a friendly dog, a beautiful building.
- **Gratitude Jar:** Write down things you're grateful for on small slips of paper and put them in a jar. When you're having a tough day, pull a few out to read.
- **Sticky-Note Wall:** Post sticky notes with things you're thankful for on a wall or mirror where you'll see them often.
- **Gratitude Playlist:** Create a playlist of songs that make you feel happy and thankful.

Gratitude in Connection

Sharing gratitude with others amplifies its effects.

- **Give Specific Compliments:** Instead of "You're great," try "I was so grateful for how you explained that concept in the meeting. It really helped me understand."
- **Praise Someone Behind Their Back:** Tell a manager how much you appreciate a colleague, or tell a friend how wonderful their partner is.
- **Start a Gratitude Circle:** At work or with family, take turns sharing one thing you're grateful for that week.

When Gratitude Feels Hard

Sometimes, it's difficult to feel grateful, especially when you're struggling. The key is authenticity. Don't force yourself to feel something you don't. On hard days, aim for tiny, undeniably true things: "I am grateful for this soft blanket." "I am grateful I have a bed to lie in." Pair this practice with self-compassion, acknowledging that it's okay to feel sad or angry while still noticing a small good thing.

Make It Stick

- **Habit Stack:** Link your gratitude practice to something you already do, like brushing your teeth or brewing coffee.
- **Set Reminders:** Use a phone alarm or a sticky note to prompt your practice at the same time each day.

Gratitude is a practice, not a feeling you have to wait for. It's a lens you can choose to look through, helping you find the light even on the cloudiest days.

Shift 26

- Hike

- E.K. perceives hiking as a calming and restorative activity.

When E.K suggested a hike, my first thought was, "I barely have the energy to get off the sofa, let alone climb a hill." But she insisted it would be good for me.

And so I hiked…

I invited MT to join me on the Crowders trail. We walked a quiet path that day and laughed over silly stories. Although I've been tired after hiking, I've had some good laughs when I've done it with a friend or companion. When we got back to the car, my legs were weary, but I was feeling lighter. E.K. was right; hiking is a calming and restorative activity, a way to physically walk yourself back to a lighter state of mind.

Why Hiking Helps Your Mood

Hiking is a powerful antidote to a low mood for several reasons. The rhythmic movement of walking helps to release physical tension stored in your body from stress and anxiety. Your muscles get to work, your blood gets pumping, and your brain releases endorphins, those wonderful natural mood-lifters.

Being in nature also has a unique effect on our minds. The theory of "attention restoration" suggests that natural environments, with their soft fascinations like rustling leaves and shifting clouds, allow our directed attention to rest and recover. This is a welcome break from the mental fatigue and rumination that often accompany sadness. The sunlight you soak up helps support your body's circadian rhythm and boosts serotonin production, both of which are crucial for a stable, positive mood.

Moreover, a hike provides a tangible sense of accomplishment. Choosing a trail, navigating it, and reaching a destination - even just a bend in the path or a specific tree - rebuilds a feeling of agency and competence. And when you hike with a friend, the shared experience adds another layer. The easy conversation, the comfortable silences, and the shared laughter help your nervous systems co-regulate, creating a powerful feeling of safety and connection.

How to Start and Keep It Doable

The key to restorative hiking is to make it accessible, not arduous.

- **Choose Your Trail Wisely:** Look for trails rated as "easy." Use apps or local park websites that show elevation gain; a flatter trail is perfect for low-energy days.
- **Use Time Boxes:** Don't commit to a 5-mile trek. Say, "Let's walk for 20 minutes and see how we feel." You can use a 20-minute out, 20-minute back model (40 minutes total) or plan for a 90-minute loop.
- **Pace Over Performance:** Let go of any need to be fast. The right speed is a "talkable pace," where you can hold a conversation without getting breathless.
- **Gear Basics:** You don't need expensive equipment. Start with comfortable, supportive shoes, clothes you can move in, and a small backpack for essentials.
- **Snacks and Hydration:** Pack more water than you think you'll need, and bring an easy-to-eat snack with some protein or natural sugar, like a handful of nuts, a piece of fruit, or a granola bar.

Safety Is Self-Care

Ensuring you are safe on the trail allows you to relax and reap the benefits.

- **Tell Someone:** Let a friend or family member know where you are going and when you expect to be back.
- **Check the Weather:** A quick look at the forecast can help you dress appropriately and avoid being caught in a storm.
- **Protect Yourself:** Wear sunscreen, a hat, and bug spray if needed.
- **Pacing and Turnaround Time:** Decide on a turnaround time before you start (e.g., "We'll head back at 45 minutes, no matter where we are"). This prevents you from going too far and getting exhausted.
- **Wildlife and Trail Etiquette:** Be aware of your surroundings, give animals plenty of space, and stick to the marked trail.

Hiking with a Friend: Making it Joyful

Sharing the path can amplify the restorative effects.

- **Shared Playlist:** Create a playlist for the drive to the trailhead to set the mood.
- **"Rose/Bud/Thorn" Check-in:** As you walk, take turns sharing a "rose" (something good), a "bud" (something you're looking forward to), and a "thorn" (a challenge).
- **Photo Prompts:** Give yourselves a fun, low-pressure task, like "find three different

kinds of leaves" or "take a picture of something that makes you smile."

- **Pockets of Silence:** Agree that it's okay to walk in comfortable silence. This takes the pressure off feeling like you have to entertain each other.
- **Snack Tradition:** Make a specific snack your "official hiking snack" that you always share at the halfway point.

When a Full Hike Is Too Much

On days when even an easy trail feels like too much, you can still find restoration in nature.

- **Urban Trails:** Explore a paved path along a river or through a city park.
- **Park Loops:** Walk a few gentle laps around your local park.
- **Stair Walks:** Find a public staircase and walk up and down a few times, focusing on your breath.
- **The Sit-Spot:** Simply take a book or a journal to a green space and sit for 20 minutes, soaking in the sights and sounds.

Your Invitation to the Trail

The path to feeling better doesn't have to be complicated. It can be as simple as putting one foot in front of the other on a patch of dirt. I invite you to plan one gentle, restorative walk for yourself this week. Use this simple checklist: Pick an easy trail or park. Choose a time box (even just 20 minutes). Tell someone your plan. Pack a water bottle and a small snack. Then, go. Go at your own pace.

May your spirit feel lighter.

Shift 27

- Exercise

- M.N. likes to exercise, which leaves her feeling energized and clear-headed.

Whether lifting weights or e-biking, exercise provides physical and emotional relief.

The idea of exercise doesn't always sound like fun. But I've learned to reframe it. It's not about punishing my body; it's about giving my mind a dose of powerful medicine. Whether it's the focused effort of lifting weights or the simple joy of walking, I've discovered that movement provides both physical and emotional relief. It's a way to shake off the tension and quiet the noise in my head.

The benefits of moving your body are immediate. When you exercise, your brain releases endorphins and serotonin, which are natural mood-lifters. This is often called a "runner's high," but you don't have to run to feel it. A brisk walk or a dance session in your living room can trigger the same positive chemical cascade. Movement is also a way to physically offload stress. When you feel anxious or angry, your body holds that tension in your muscles. Exercise gives that energy a place to go, leaving you feeling calmer and more grounded.

This physical activity improves sleep quality, which is often disrupted by sadness and stress. It also rebuilds a sense of body confidence and agency. When you feel helpless, proving to yourself that you can lift a weight, hold a yoga pose, or walk a little farther than last week is a powerful reminder of your own strength. It interrupts the cycle of rumination by demanding your presence and focus, giving your worried mind a much-needed break.

A Menu of Mood-Boosting Movements

The best exercise is the one you will actually do. Find something that feels good, or at least interesting, to you.

- **Walking:** The ultimate accessible exercise. A walk outdoors offers sunlight and fresh air, while a treadmill walk or laps around a mall work perfectly on bad weather days.
- **E-Biking or Cycling:** E-bikes are fantastic because they allow you to go farther and tackle hills with less effort, making it more about the joy of movement and scenery than a grueling workout. Traditional cycling offers a similar freedom.

- **Strength Training:** You don't need a gym. Start with bodyweight exercises like squats, push-ups against a wall, and planks. Adding a pair of light dumbbells can provide a tangible sense of getting stronger.
- **Yoga, Stretching, and Mobility:** These practices are perfect for low-energy days. They connect you to your breath, gently release muscle tension, and calm the nervous system.
- **Dancing:** Put on your favorite music and move freely in your living room for three songs. It's a pure expression of joy and a fantastic stress-buster.
- **Swimming or Aqua Aerobics:** The feeling of being supported by water is incredibly soothing and low-impact on your joints.
- **Low-Impact Cardio:** Machines like the elliptical or rower provide a great cardiovascular workout without the pounding of running, which is ideal if you have joint pain.

Making Movement Doable and Kind

Starting is the hardest part. Let's make it easy and gentle.

- **Use Time Boxes:** Don't commit to an hour. Tell yourself, "I'll just move for 10 minutes." Often, once you start, you'll want to continue. Set a timer for 5, 10, or 20 minutes. Ten is enough.

- **Aim for a "Talkable Pace":** You should be able to hold a conversation while you're moving. This is a good indicator that you're working at a sustainable, moderate intensity (around a 4-6 on a 1-10 scale of perceived exertion).
- **Warm-Up and Cool-Down:** Start with 3-5 minutes of lighter movement (like walking in place) and end with 3-5 minutes of gentle stretching.
- **Find Joyful Cues:** What makes it fun? A great playlist, a beautiful park, a podcast, or a friend to walk with. Pair your movement with something you love. When you're with a buddy, set the tone with, "Let's keep it easy today."

Your Invitation to Move

You don't need to transform your life overnight. You just need to take one small step. This week, I invite you to choose one activity from this list and try it for just 10 or 20 minutes. Notice how you feel before you start, and notice how you feel after. Don't judge the performance; just celebrate the act of showing up for yourself. You are giving your body and mind a gift - a moment of relief, a spark of energy, and a reminder of your own resilience.

Shift 28

- Changing Scenery

- D.B. shares the value of exploring new places or engaging in new activities for a fresh perspective.

There is immense value in exploring new places or engaging in new activities for gaining a fresh perspective. I've found this to be profoundly true in my own life. Sometimes, just changing my location helps with a mood shift. It doesn't have to be a grand vacation; even walking down a different street in my own neighborhood can feel like hitting a reset button for my mind. When we feel stuck in a loop of sadness or worry, intentionally seeking out novelty can be the gentle jolt we need to see our world, and ourselves, in a new light.

This isn't just a feeling; there's a real science to it. Our brains are wired to pay attention to new things. When you experience something novel, your brain releases a small burst of dopamine, a neurotransmitter linked to motivation and reward. This creates a feeling of engagement and interest that can temporarily override feelings of apathy. Exploring a new place or trying a new activity forces your brain to stop ruminating on old problems and focus on the present moment. You have to navigate, observe, and process new information, which effectively breaks the cycle of stale, repetitive thoughts. This simple act restores a sense of agency and possibility, reminding you that there is still a wide, interesting world out there, full of things yet to be discovered.

Practical Ways to Find a Fresh Perspective

You can find novelty everywhere, on any budget and with any amount of energy. It's about cultivating a spirit of gentle curiosity.

Micro-Location Shifts (5–30 minutes)

- **Work from a New Window:** If you work from home, move your laptop to a different window for an hour. Notice the different light and view.
- **Visit a New Park Bench:** Go to your local park and sit on a bench you've never used before.
- **Take a "Left Turn Only" Walk:** Leave your home and take only left turns for 15 minutes, then find your way back. You'll be amazed at what you discover.
- **Browse a Different Aisle:** Go to your usual grocery store but spend ten minutes walking slowly down an aisle you always skip.

Local Explorations (1-3 hours)

- **Become a Neighborhood Tourist:** Choose a neighborhood in your town you don't know well and spend an afternoon walking its streets. Pop into a local coffee shop or browse a small store.
- **Explore Your Local Library:** Go beyond the book stacks. See if they have a local history section, a seed library, or art on display.
- **Visit a Public Garden or Conservatory:** Surround yourself with the sights and smells of plants you don't normally see.
- **Go on a "Color Hunt":** Choose a color and spend an hour taking pictures of everything you see in that shade.

New Activities (Low-Cost to Moderate)

- **Try a New Recipe:** Choose a simple recipe from a cuisine you've never cooked before. Focus on the new smells and textures.
- **Listen to a Different Genre of Music:** Use a streaming service to explore a genre you know nothing about, from classical to cumbia to jazz.
- **Learn a Simple Skill on YouTube:** Spend 30 minutes learning how to do something new, like juggle one ball, fold an origami crane, or learn a basic magic trick.

- **Drop into a Community Class:** Many community centers or studios offer a free or low-cost first class for yoga, pottery, or dance.

Making It Doable

- **Set a "Freshness Budget":** This could be a small amount of money ($10 for a new coffee shop) or a block of time (one hour every Saturday) dedicated to novelty.
- **Use Prompts:** Give yourself a simple mission, like "same street, new eyes." Walk your usual route but look up at the rooftops instead of at the ground.
- **Prep a "Go-Bag":** Keep a small bag with a water bottle, a snack, a notebook, and a transit pass ready. This reduces the friction of getting out the door for a spontaneous exploration.
- **Keep It Safe and Comfortable:** Wear comfortable shoes. Tell someone where you're going if you're exploring a new area. The goal is gentle discovery, not a stressful ordeal.

Shaking up your routine doesn't have to be overwhelming. By inviting small doses of novelty into your life, you create space for your mind to breathe. You remind yourself that change is possible, that new things are waiting, and that your perspective is not fixed. It's a gentle, powerful way to find your way back to a good feeling.

Shift 29

- Listen to Uplifting Content

- B.C. suggests listening to inspirational and positive podcasts for encouragement.

I started with some Jay Shetty content and discovered a world of uplifting audio. Sometimes it's a radio show, or even a TED Talk or an audiobook.

Since going blind, my dad listens to a lot of audiobooks, and it has become a vital source of connection and engagement for him. Consciously choosing what we listen to can be one of the most passive yet powerful ways to shift our inner state. Uplifting content guides us toward a better mood.

Why Uplifting Audio Works

Listening to positive content does more than just distract us; it actively reshapes our emotional and mental environment. It works by shifting our attention. When we are caught in a cycle of worry, a compelling story or an interesting idea gives our brain something new and constructive to focus on. The human voice itself has a powerful effect. A calm, kind, or enthusiastic voice can help regulate our own nervous system through a process called co-regulation, making us feel safer and more settled.

Stories of resilience and hope are particularly potent. Hearing how someone else navigated a difficult time fosters a sense of shared humanity and possibility, making our own challenges feel more manageable. Many podcasts and talks also offer practical reframing tools, helping us see a situation from a different, more empowering angle. Best of all, audio is incredibly habit-friendly. Because it's hands-free, we can easily weave it into parts of our day that are already established - our morning walk, our commute, or while doing household chores.

How to Listen Intentionally

To get the most out of your listening, it helps to be mindful. Use "audio anchors" by pairing a podcast with a specific daily activity. Maybe your morning coffee is your time for a 10-minute motivational talk, or you listen to a storytelling show while you fold laundry. You can also vary your listening style. Sometimes, active listening is best - sitting with a notebook and really absorbing the ideas. Other times, passive listening is perfect. For example, the audio can just be in the background.

Consider whether you need to match your mood or lift it. On a very low day, a deeply empathetic and gentle voice might feel more comforting than a high-energy motivational speaker. It's also important to set boundaries to avoid being overwhelmed. You don't need to listen constantly. A single 20-minute episode can be more than enough to provide a lasting boost.

A Menu of Uplifting Content to Explore

The world of audio is vast. Here are a few places to start your exploration.

Podcasts:

- **Inspirational Interviews:** These shows feature deep conversations about life, purpose, and overcoming challenges.
  - *On Purpose with Jay Shetty*: Explores wisdom and personal growth with a wide range of guests.
  - *The Good Life Project*: Features inspiring stories from all walks of life.
  - *Super Soul with Oprah Winfrey*: Oprah's personal selection of her interviews with thought-leaders and spiritual luminaries.
- **Science of Well-being:** These podcasts break down the science of happiness and provide evidence-based tips.
  - *The Happiness Lab with Dr. Laurie Santos*: Yale professor Dr. Santos

shares surprising research on what makes us happy.

- ○ *Ten Percent Happier with Dan Harris*: Explores meditation and mindfulness with a relatable, skeptical approach.
- **Spirituality & Creativity:** Gentle shows that explore the deeper aspects of life and the creative spirit.
  - ○ *On Being with Krista Tippett*: A Peabody Award-winning conversation about the big questions of meaning.
  - ○ *The Creative Pep Talk Podcast*: Helps creative people find their path and stay motivated.

TED and TEDx Talks:
Search for themes like "resilience," "happiness," "creativity," or "connection." Brené Brown's talks on vulnerability are a wonderful starting point. These short, powerful talks are perfect for a quick dose of inspiration.

Radio Shows and Audiobooks:
Look for call-in shows focused on encouragement or storytelling programs like *The Moth Radio Hour*. For audiobooks, consider memoirs about overcoming adversity, fiction with a lot of heart, or short wisdom books.

- *Man's Search for Meaning* by Viktor E. Frankl

- *Braiding Sweetgrass* by Robin Wall Kimmerer
- *Year of Yes* by Shonda Rhimes

Making Audio Accessible

For those with visual impairments, like my dad, audio is a lifeline. Most podcast apps and audiobook services have built-in accessibility features. Get comfortable with adjusting playback speed, using voice commands like "Hey Siri, play *The Daily* podcast," and using smart speakers for hands-free control.

By curating your own audio environment, you are taking an active role in protecting your peace and cultivating a more hopeful mindset. You are choosing the voices you allow into your head and heart. Choose wisely, and let them be kind.

Shift 30

- Caregiving

- B.N. enjoys connecting with others through caregiving.

When we think of "caregiving," our minds often jump to monumental tasks such as full-time nursing for an ailing parent or raising young children. But care is a much broader, more beautiful concept. It lives in the small, quiet moments: dropping off a container of soup for a neighbor who's had a rough week, texting a friend to say "I'm thinking of you," or watering a coworker's plants while they're away. I've learned that one of the most reliable antidotes to the isolating ache of sadness is to turn my focus outward. Engaging in acts of care, no matter how small, connects us to others in a deeply meaningful way and, in doing so, brings a surprising sense of peace to our own hearts.

How Caring for Others Calms Our Own Spirit

Giving care is a powerful way to soothe our own internal turmoil. It provides a sense of purpose when we feel adrift, anchoring us to a tangible, helpful action. When we offer comfort to someone, our own nervous system often responds in kind. This process of co-regulation, where your calm presence helps soothe another, can also lower your own stress levels. The act of caring shifts our perspective away from our own looping thoughts and worries, reminding us of a world beyond our own pain and fostering a sense of gratitude for what we can offer.

This act of giving creates meaning. It transforms our feelings of helplessness into agency, proving that even when we are struggling, we still have the capacity to make a positive impact. I've found that this builds a quiet confidence. It's a gentle reminder that we are all part of an ecosystem of support, and our small contributions matter.

Practical Ways to Connect Through Care

Connecting through care doesn't have to be draining. You can choose actions that match your energy level and schedule.

Micro-Acts of Care

- **The Check-in Text:** Send a simple, no-reply-needed message: "Just passed that park we like and thought of you. Sending a wave!"
- **The Digital Drop-off:** Share a link to an article, a funny video, or a song you think a friend would enjoy with a note like, "This made me smile and I thought it might for you, too."

- **The Five-Minute Favor:** Offer to do a tiny task for a friend or family member, like taking out their trash cans, refilling their water bottle, or proofreading a single email.

Ongoing Support Rhythms

- **Weekly Call:** Set a recurring time each week for a short phone call with someone who might be lonely. It provides a reliable point of connection for both of you.
- **Shared Meal Prep:** Get together with a friend once a week to cook a big batch of something simple, like soup or chili, and split it. You get a few meals prepped and enjoy the companionship.
- **Companion Visits:** Offer to simply be present with someone. Read a book in the same room as an elderly relative or sit with a new parent while the baby sleeps. Your quiet company is a gift.

Community and Intergenerational Care

- **Join a Mutual Aid Group:** These local networks connect neighbors to share resources and support, from grocery runs to yard work.
- **Volunteer for a Cause:** Find a cause you care about and offer a few hours a month. Animal

shelters, food banks, and community gardens are often looking for help.

- **Connect Across Generations:** Offer to help an older neighbor with technology, or ask them to teach you a skill they have, like knitting or gardening.

The Other Side of the Coin: Receiving Care with Grace

Just as important as giving care is learning how to receive it. This can be difficult, as we often feel like a burden. But allowing someone to care for you is also a gift; it lets them experience the peace and purpose that comes from helping.

When a friend offers, "Let me know if you need anything," try responding with a specific, small request: "Could you actually pick up milk for me the next time you're at the store?" or "I'd love a 10-minute phone call tomorrow just to hear a friendly voice." Accepting help is not a sign of weakness; it's an act of trust that strengthens your connection. It completes the circle of care, reminding us that we are all worthy of support.

Simple Rituals to Bring Calm to Care

To keep caregiving from becoming another source of stress, infuse it with small, calming rituals.

- **The Centering Breath:** Before you make a call or drop off a meal, take three slow, deep breaths. Set an intention: "May this act bring comfort."
- **The Music Cue:** Play a specific, calming piece of music while you are doing a caring task, like cooking for someone.
- **The Closing Ritual:** After you've spent time with someone, take a moment in your car or on your walk home to acknowledge what you gave and received.

Your Invitation to Connect

Caring for others is a practice that can gently guide you out of the fog of your own sadness and into the warmth of human connection.

This week, I invite you to try one small act of care. It doesn't need to be grand. You could text an old friend a happy memory, offer to water your neighbor's plant, or simply ask the grocery clerk how their day is going and truly listen to the answer. Notice how that small offering feels in your own heart.

In reaching out to another, you may just find the peace you've been looking for.

Shift 31

- Volunteering

- E.S. enjoys volunteering for personal renewal.

Volunteering isn't just about giving back to the community; it's a powerful act of personal renewal that can restore our sense of purpose and lift our spirits when we need it most.

Why Volunteering Helps Us Heal

Dedicating our time to a cause larger than ourselves has a remarkable effect on our well-being. It creates a powerful sense of belonging. When we work alongside others toward a shared goal, we build an immediate social connection that can combat feelings of loneliness and isolation. The simple act of being part of a team, even for a few hours, helps our nervous system co-regulate, making us feel safer and more connected.

Volunteering provides a clear sense of purpose and agency. On days when we feel helpless, contributing in a meaningful way restores our belief in our own ability to make a difference. This boost in self-esteem is a powerful antidote to a low mood. It also shifts our perspective. Working with people facing different challenges can foster deep gratitude for our own circumstances and pull us out of the habit of rumination. Depending on the role, it can also offer skill growth or precious time in nature, both of which are known to enhance mental health.

Safety and Sustainability: Volunteering Wisely

To ensure your experience is restorative, it's important to approach it with intention and care.

- **Choose an Aligned Cause:** Pick something that genuinely matters to you, whether it's animal welfare, environmental conservation, or supporting children. Your intrinsic motivation will make the experience more meaningful.
- **Vet the Organization:** Look for established non-profits with clear missions and good reviews. A well-organized group will provide a better, safer experience.
- **Set Boundaries:** Be realistic about the time and energy you can commit. It's better to offer two hours a month consistently than to promise ten and burn out. It's okay to say, "I can help with this, but I'm not available for that."
- **Seek Role Clarity:** Make sure you understand what is expected of you. A clear role prevents confusion and stress.
- **Pace Yourself:** Choose roles that match your physical and social energy levels. If you're an

introvert, a quiet data-entry role might be more renewing than a bustling event.

- **Basic Precautions:** Be aware of your surroundings, especially if volunteering in an unfamiliar area. Using a buddy system for your first few times can be helpful. Reputable organizations will have their own safety protocols and may require background checks for certain roles.

Ways to Volunteer for Every Energy Level

There is a volunteer opportunity to fit every schedule and capacity.

Micro-Volunteering (5-30 minutes, often remote)

- Use an app like Be My Eyes to assist a visually impaired person with a quick task.
- Transcribe historical documents for a museum online.
- Write a positive review for a local non-profit you admire.

Low-Energy and Local Roles

- Sort donations at a food pantry or clothing drive.
- Write letters or cards to residents of a nursing home or to soldiers stationed overseas.

- Help with simple administrative tasks like stuffing envelopes at a non-profit office.

People-Centered Roles

- Become a friendly caller for isolated seniors.
- Mentor a young person through an organization like Big Brothers Big Sisters.
- Read stories to children at your local library or a hospital.

Outdoor and Service Roles

- Join a park or beach cleanup day.
- Help out at a community garden; weeding, watering, or harvesting.
- Socialize with animals at a local shelter.

Skills-Based and Virtual Volunteering

- Offer your professional skills (graphic design, writing, accounting) to a non-profit.
- Tutor students online in a subject you know well.
- Help seniors learn how to use technology through a local community center.

Getting Started: Your Path to Renewal

1. **Reflect:** What causes touch your heart? What skills or time can you offer?

2. **Research:** Use websites like VolunteerMatch or Idealist, or simply search for "volunteer opportunities" in your city.
3. **Reach Out:** Send an email or make a call to one organization that looks promising. A simple script: "Hi, I'm interested in volunteering. Could you tell me more about your current needs?"
4. **Start Small:** Commit to a single event or a short-term project first to see how it feels.

When we offer our time and energy to care for our community, we are also, in turn, caring for ourselves. It is a reminder that we are needed, we are connected, and we have the power to create positive change.

Shift 32

- Beach Trip

Why the Beach Helps Us Feel Better

The sense of calm we feel at the shore is backed by simple science. Our brains are positively affected by "blue spaces," natural environments dominated by water. The vast, open horizon gives our eyes a place to rest, reducing the mental fatigue caused by our screen-heavy, enclosed daily lives. The predictable sound of waves is soothing to our nervous system. It can slow our heart rate and shift us out of a "fight-or-flight" state into a more relaxed "rest-and-digest" mode.

Sunlight on our skin helps our bodies produce Vitamin D and can improve both mood and sleep. Some people find the sea breeze itself invigorating. Even the simple act of walking on sand provides a gentle workout and a grounding physical sensation, connecting us to the earth.

A Guide to Safe and Accessible Beach Days

To fully relax and enjoy the benefits, it's important to feel safe and comfortable. A little planning goes a long way.

- **Sun Safety:** The sun is strongest between 10 a.m. and 4 p.m. Plan your visit for the morning or late afternoon if possible. Always wear broad-spectrum sunscreen, a wide-brimmed hat, and sunglasses.
- **Hydration is Key:** The sun and wind can dehydrate you quickly. Bring more water than you think you'll need.
- **Water Awareness:** Pay attention to ocean conditions. Look for posted signs about rip currents and check the flag system if lifeguards are present. If you're not a strong swimmer, stay in shallow water.
- **Protect Your Feet:** Sand can get incredibly hot, and rocks or shells can be sharp. Wear sandals or water shoes.
- **Take Breaks:** Alternate between sun and shade. An umbrella, tent, or a spot near a shady pier can provide a much-needed cool-down.
- **Accessibility:** Many public beaches now offer accessibility features like wooden boardwalks that go closer to the water and beach wheelchairs with large, sand-friendly tires.

Check the local parks department website for information. Visiting during off-peak hours can also make navigating easier and less overwhelming.

A Menu of Mood-Lifting Beach Activities

Your beach trip can be as active or as restful as you need it to be. Choose an activity that matches your energy level.

Micro-Activities

- **Barefoot Grounding:** Take off your shoes and walk along the wet sand. Focus on the sensation of the earth beneath your feet.
- **Breathe with the Waves:** Sit near the water's edge and synchronize your breath with the ocean. Inhale as a wave rolls in, exhale as it recedes.
- **Gratitude Lines:** Use a finger or a piece of driftwood to write three things you are grateful for in the sand, then watch the waves wash them away.

Gentle Activities

- **Tideline Walk:** Stroll along the water's edge, letting the cool foam wash over your ankles. This is a perfect "moving meditation."

- **Beachcombing:** Walk with a gentle focus, looking for unique shells, smoothed sea glass, or interesting driftwood.
- **Sit-Spot Journaling:** Find a comfortable spot, set a timer for 20 minutes, and write about whatever comes to mind, inspired by the sights and sounds around you.

Social and Playful Fun

- **Simple Games:** A game of catch, paddle ball, or frisbee is a wonderful way to connect and get your body moving.
- **Sandcastle Building:** This playful, creative act is not just for kids. The focus and creativity are wonderfully absorbing.
- **Photo Scavenger Hunt:** Create a list with a friend: "something blue," "a perfectly round stone," "a bird in flight," and see what you can find.

Restorative Rituals

- **Sunrise or Sunset Watch:** Witnessing the sun meet the horizon over the water is a powerful, awe-inspiring ritual that costs nothing.
- **Seaside Picnic:** A simple meal tastes better with an ocean view. Pack some sandwiches, fruit, and a thermos of a favorite drink.

- **Mindful Listening:** Find a safe spot, close your eyes for five minutes, and simply listen. Try to identify all the different sounds: the waves, the birds, the wind, the distant laughter.

Rainy or Cool-Day Alternatives

- **Boardwalk Stroll:** A walk on a boardwalk or pier offers a great view and keeps your feet out of the cold, wet sand.
- **Harbor Visit:** Explore a nearby harbor, watch the boats, and enjoy the maritime atmosphere.
- **Ocean View with a Hot Drink:** Find a café with a window overlooking the water and enjoy a warm beverage while you watch the weather.

Plan Your Beach Reset

You don't need a full day to experience the healing power of the shore. I invite you to plan one small beach reset for yourself.

1. **Pick a safe time and location:** Choose a time of day that works for your energy and check the weather and tides.
2. **Pack the essentials:** Sunscreen, water, a hat, and a towel.
3. **Choose one micro-activity and one gentle activity:** Decide beforehand to simply breathe

with the waves and then take a 20-minute tideline walk.

4. **Set a turnaround time:** Give yourself permission to leave when you need to. An hour can be more than enough.

The beach is a place of perspective. It reminds us that we are small parts of something vast and beautiful, and that just like the tide, our own low moods can recede.

Shift 33

- Trusted Conversations

- N.S. finds speaking to a trusted person helpful.

There is a special kind of healing that happens when we allow someone to witness our struggle, not to fix it, but to simply be with us in it. Sharing our burden with a safe person doesn't make the burden disappear, but it makes it feel lighter, more manageable, and reminds us that we are not alone.

Why Trusted Conversations Help

When we share our feelings with a trusted person, we are doing more than just venting. We are engaging in a powerful biological and psychological process. The simple act of being in the presence of a calm, empathetic person helps regulate our own nervous system. Their steady presence can lower our heart rate and ease the physical symptoms of stress without a single word of advice.

Being truly seen and heard is validating. When someone listens and responds with, "That sounds incredibly difficult," or "I can understand why you feel that way," it confirms that our feelings are real and legitimate. This validation is a direct antidote to the shame and isolation that often accompany sadness. Talking through a problem also helps us create a coherent narrative. What feels like a chaotic mess in our head can become a structured story with a beginning, middle, and end when we say it out loud. And finally, a trusted conversation offers perspective. A friend might gently point out a strength we've overlooked or simply reflect our situation back to us in a way that makes it feel less overwhelming.

How to Know You Can Trust Someone

Trust is built over time through consistent actions. A trustworthy person doesn't have to be your oldest friend or a family member; they just need to be a safe harbor for your feelings.

Signals of a Trustworthy Person:

- **Reliability:** They do what they say they will do. Their actions match their words.
- **Confidentiality:** You have evidence that they don't share private information. They don't gossip about others, so you can trust they won't gossip about you.
- **Non-Judgment:** They listen to your experiences without making you feel wrong or foolish. They listen with curiosity, not criticism.

- **Empathy:** They try to understand your feelings from your point of view, even if they haven't had the exact same experience.
- **Good Boundaries:** They are clear about their own limits and respect yours. They can say "no" gracefully.

Red Flags to Watch For:

- They gossip or share others' private stories.
- They consistently minimize your feelings with phrases like, "It's not that bad," or "Just look on the bright side."
- They immediately jump into "advice-only" mode without first listening.
- They are frequently unreliable or cancel plans last minute.

How to Start and Guide the Conversation

Initiating a vulnerable conversation can feel awkward. Using simple scripts can help create a safe container for both of you.

- **Get Consent First:** Before you dive in, check if the other person has the capacity to listen.
  - *"Hey, do you have space to listen to something a bit heavy? No pressure if now's not a good time."*

- "I'm going through something and could use a friend to talk to. Are you free for a call later this week?"

- **State What You Need:** Be clear about whether you want a listener or a problem-solver.
  - "I don't really need advice right now, I just need to get this off my chest. Would you be willing to just listen?"
  - "I feel stuck and would love to brainstorm some ideas with you after I explain the situation."

- **Use a Time Box:** To keep the conversation from feeling overwhelming for either of you, you can set a gentle boundary.
  - "Could we just talk for about 15 minutes? I think that would really help."

- **Check In:** If you feel a mismatch, it's okay to gently redirect.
  - "I appreciate you trying to find solutions, but for now, it would help most just to know you hear me."

Boundaries and Aftercare

Protecting your energy is key. You don't have to share every detail of a situation to feel understood. You can share the emotional core without revealing parts that feel too private. After a heavy conversation, practice some simple aftercare. Drink a glass of water, take a few deep breaths, or go for a short walk to ground yourself.

What If You Don't Have Someone?

Many people feel they lack a person they can truly confide in. If this is you, you are not alone, and there are wonderful alternatives.

- **Support Lines:** Helplines are staffed by trained listeners who are there to provide immediate, confidential support.
- **Peer Support Groups:** Finding a group of people with a shared experience (like grief, chronic illness, or caregiving) can be incredibly validating.
- **Therapy:** A therapist is a trained, professional trusted person who can provide skilled support and tools.
- **Journaling or Voice Notes:** The act of speaking your truth, even to yourself, can be very powerful. Record a voice note on your

phone as if you were talking to a compassionate friend.

Your Invitation to Connect

True connection is one of our deepest human needs. This week, I invite you to take one small step toward a trusted conversation.

1. **Identify one person:** Think of someone in your life who has shown signals of being a good listener.
2. **Plan one micro-share:** You don't have to share your deepest secret. Start small. Try sharing a minor frustration or a small worry, using one of the scripts above.

Notice how it feels to be heard, even for just a few minutes. In that shared space, you can find a moment of peace, a bit of clarity, and the quiet strength that comes from knowing you don't have to carry it all by yourself.

Shift 34

- Sleep

- H.M. suggests simply catching up on sleep.

I used to think of sleep as a luxury, the first thing to be sacrificed when life got busy. It took years of waking up irritable and overwhelmed for me to understand that good sleep isn't a luxury. It's the very foundation of a stable mood. I remember one particular week when I was burning the candle at both ends; by Friday, a minor inconvenience like spilling tea felt like a catastrophe. It wasn't the tea. It was the accumulated sleep debt that had frayed my nerves and left me with no emotional buffer. A good night's rest is like a system reset for the mind, a cornerstone of calm that we simply can't do without.

Why Your Brain Needs Sleep to Be Happy

When you sleep, your brain is doing far more than just powering down. It's performing critical maintenance that directly impacts your emotional well-being.

One of the most important jobs happens in the connection between your amygdala (the brain's emotional alarm center) and your prefrontal cortex (the rational, decision-making part). When you're well-rested, these two areas are in constant communication, allowing you to respond to situations thoughtfully. When you're sleep-deprived, that connection weakens. Your amygdala goes into overdrive, making you react more impulsively and emotionally, while the logical part of your brain struggles to keep up.

Sleep also plays a vital role in managing key brain chemicals. It helps regulate neurotransmitters like serotonin and dopamine, which are crucial for feelings of well-being, motivation, and pleasure. Furthermore, it helps reset your body's stress response system by regulating cortisol levels. Without proper sleep, cortisol can remain elevated, leaving you feeling perpetually stressed and anxious. During deep REM sleep, your brain also processes the emotional events of the day, helping to file them away and reduce their emotional charge. This is why a problem that feels overwhelming at midnight can often feel more manageable in the morning.

Signs Your Sleep Is Affecting Your Mood

Sometimes the connection isn't obvious. You might just feel "off" without knowing why. Here are a few signs that poor sleep might be the culprit:

- **High irritability and low frustration tolerance:** Small annoyances feel like huge personal attacks.
- **"Sticky" negative thoughts:** It's harder to shake off worries or pessimistic thinking.
- **Social withdrawal:** Interacting with others feels exhausting and overwhelming.
- **Increased cravings for carbohydrates and sugar:** Your tired brain is desperately seeking a quick energy source.

Gentle Supports for Better Sleep

You can't force yourself to sleep, but as I often tell myself, "I can't force sleep, but I can create the conditions for it." The goal is to send your body consistent signals that it's time to wind down.

- **Anchor Your Day with Light:** Try to get 5-10 minutes of daylight within an hour of waking. This helps set your body's internal clock.
- **Keep a Consistent Wake-Up Time:** Even on weekends, try to wake up within the same one-hour window. This is more powerful than a consistent bedtime.
- **Create a Wind-Down Ritual:** An hour before bed, transition to calming activities. Dim the lights, put away screens, listen to soft music, or read a physical book.

- **Mind Your Timing:** Avoid caffeine after noon and limit alcohol in the evening. While alcohol might make you feel drowsy, it disrupts sleep quality later in the night.
- **Create a Sanctuary:** Make your bedroom a cool, dark, and quiet haven. Use blackout curtains or an eye mask if needed. A hot bath or shower 1-2 hours before bed can also help by lowering your core body temperature afterward, which signals sleep.
- **Perform a "Worry Dump":** If your mind races at night, spend 10 minutes before your wind-down ritual writing down everything you're worried about. This gets it out of your head and onto the page.

Quick Resets for Bad Nights

Everyone has a bad night of sleep now and then. Instead of panicking, be compassionate with yourself.

- **The Strategic Nap:** If you need to nap, keep it to 20-30 minutes in the early afternoon to avoid disrupting your nighttime sleep.
- **Non-Sleep Deep Rest:** If you can't nap, simply lie down in a quiet room for 10-20 minutes and listen to a guided meditation. This can be deeply restorative even without sleep.
- **Compassion Scripts:** Tell yourself, "One bad night won't ruin me. I will be gentle with myself

today and trust my body will get the rest it
needs tonight."

When to Seek More Help

While these strategies can help immensely, some
issues require professional support. Talk to a doctor if
you experience persistent insomnia (trouble falling or
staying asleep most nights), loud snoring (which could
be a sign of sleep apnea), an irresistible urge to move
your legs at night (restless leg syndrome), or if your
low mood doesn't improve with better sleep.

Sleep is not a passive activity; it is an active and
essential process of restoration. By treating it with the
respect it deserves, you are giving your mind the
greatest possible gift: the space to heal, rebalance,
and find its way back to a state of calm.

Shift 35

- Organizing

- M.H. finds joy in organizing spaces.

After clearing my desk, I felt a renewed sense of focus...

Why Organizing Your Space Helps Your Mind

The link between our external environment and our internal state is incredibly strong. Decluttering and organizing aren't just about tidiness; they are powerful acts of self-care that directly impact our mood and focus. When our eyes scan a cluttered space, our brains have to process all that "visual noise," which consumes mental energy and leads to fatigue. Each item can also act as a tiny reminder of an unfinished task, pinging our brains with a low-grade hum of stress.

The simple act of sorting and organizing gives us a tangible sense of control and agency, which is a powerful antidote to feeling helpless or overwhelmed. As you move your body and complete small tasks; like wiping down a counter or putting away a pile of laundry - your brain releases a little bit of dopamine, the neurotransmitter associated with reward and motivation. This creates a positive feedback loop. A clear space also creates a clearer path for your brain. When your environment has distinct cues for tasks (like a clear desk for working or a tidy kitchen for cooking), it's easier for your mind to get started and stay focused.

A Gentle Framework for Decluttering

The thought of organizing an entire house can be paralyzing. The key is to start small and be kind to yourself.

- **The 10-Minute Reset:** Set a timer for just ten minutes and tackle one small area. You'll be amazed at what you can accomplish. It's about building momentum, not achieving perfection.
- **One Surface at a Time:** Don't try to declutter a whole room. Just focus on one surface, like the kitchen table, the entryway console, or your nightstand.
- **The Five-Box Method:** Grab five boxes or bags and label them: Keep, Relocate (for items that belong in another room), Recycle, Trash, and Donate. This makes decision-making much faster.
- **The Container Rule:** If a category of items (like pens or spices) won't fit in its designated container, it's time to pare down.

Micro-Habits to Stay Organized

Maintaining a clear space is about creating small, sustainable habits.

- **The Closing Ritual:** At the end of the day, spend five minutes putting things back where they belong. Wipe down your desk or kitchen counter.
- **The "Inbox" Basket:** Designate one basket near your entryway for mail, keys, and other stray items that come into the house. Sort through it once a day.
- **The Two-Minute Rule:** If a task takes less than two minutes (like putting a dish in the dishwasher or hanging up your coat), do it immediately.
- **The Weekly Reset:** Choose one 15-minute slot each week to quickly tidy up high-traffic areas.

Quick Wins: Room-by-Room

Need a fast mood boost? Tackle one of these high-impact zones.

- **Desk:** Clear everything off, wipe it down, and only put back the essentials.
- **Entryway:** Hang up coats, line up shoes, and sort the mail.

- **Kitchen Counters:** Put away appliances, clear food items, and give the counter a good wipe.
- **Nightstand:** Remove old glasses, books you've finished, and anything that isn't essential for your wind-down routine.
- **Bathroom Counter:** Store away toiletries you don't use daily.

Mindset and Boundaries

Be compassionate with yourself. Progress is more important than perfection. If you struggle with sentimental items, create one "memory box" to store them in, rather than letting them clutter your living space. Recognize decision fatigue - if you start feeling overwhelmed, it's okay to stop and try again tomorrow.

For those with neurodiversity or low-energy conditions, the goal isn't a minimalist home; it's a functional space that supports your well-being.

Adapt these rules to work for you.

Shift 36

- Read

- A.S. turns to a good book for comfort and escape.

There are days when the world feels too loud, too heavy, and too demanding. On those days, I've learned that one of the kindest things I can do for myself is to turn to a good book for comfort and escape. I remember curling up on the sofa with a simple heartfelt novel, and within minutes, the anxieties of the day began to fade. The four walls of my room dissolved, replaced by a charming English village or sisterhood. For a little while, I wasn't just me; I was a detective solving a mystery or a traveler on an epic quest. In losing myself in a story, I found a little piece of calm.

Why Reading Soothes the Mind

Reading is more than just a hobby; it's a powerful tool for mental and emotional well-being. When we immerse ourselves in a book, we shift our attention away from the cycle of our own worries. This simple act of focusing on a narrative gives our minds a much-needed break. Studies have shown that reading can reduce stress levels significantly, sometimes even more effectively than listening to music or taking a walk.

The voice of a story, whether it's the one in your head or the narrator of an audiobook, can be incredibly regulating. It provides a steady, calming presence that helps soothe a frazzled nervous system. Stories also build empathy, allowing us to step into someone else's shoes and see the world from a different perspective. This can make our own problems feel less isolating and more manageable. When we get lost in a truly compelling book, we enter a "flow state" - a state of complete absorption where time seems to fly by. This is the ultimate mental escape, and it's deeply restorative. Finally, reading a physical book before bed can improve sleep quality by helping you wind down without the disruptive blue light from screens.

How to Build a Soothing Reading Ritual

To get the most out of your reading time, create a ritual that signals to your brain it's time to relax.

- **Use Time Boxes:** You don't need hours. Start with just 15 minutes a day. Set a timer and give yourself permission to do nothing but read until it goes off.
- **Create a Cozy Setup:** Find a comfortable chair, grab a soft blanket, and make a warm

drink. A dedicated, cozy spot makes reading feel like a special treat.
- **Put Your Phone Out of Reach:** The biggest enemy of a good reading session is the digital distraction. Put your phone in another room or turn it on silent.
- **Try an Audiobook Walk:** Pair a gentle walk with an audiobook. The combination of light movement and storytelling can be incredibly calming.
- **Use Your Library:** Place holds on books you want to read through your local library's app. The anticipation of a new book arriving is part of the fun!

Making Reading Accessible

Everyone deserves to enjoy a good book. Many resources are available to make reading easier. Libraries offer large-print editions and a huge selection of audiobooks through free apps like Libby. E-readers allow you to adjust font size and style, and some, like Kindle, have the OpenDyslexic font available to make reading easier for those with dyslexia.

A book is a quiet friend, a wise teacher, and a safe harbor. By opening its pages, you open a door to a world of adventure and perspective.

Shift 37

- Knitting and Crocheting

- C.A. recommends knitting or crocheting as creative, calming activities.

I tried but my skills are just not up to par...

Here are some notes from my research.

Why Stitching Lifts the Spirit

The simple act of knitting or crocheting has an effect on our mental well-being. The repetitive motion of creating stitches is a form of active meditation. It helps to activate the parasympathetic nervous system, which is our body's "rest and digest" mode, calming our heart rate and lowering stress hormones.

Focusing on your hands and the flow of the yarn pulls your attention into the present moment, creating a "flow state" where worries about the past and future can fade away. The tactile comfort of working with soft fibers is inherently soothing. And unlike many tasks in our digital lives, knitting and crocheting provide visible, tangible progress. Each completed row is a small win, delivering a little hit of dopamine that motivates you to keep going. The practice offers opportunities to create heartfelt gifts for others, which amplifies feelings of purpose and joy.

Getting Started

The yarn aisle can be an intimidating place. The key to starting is to keep it incredibly simple.

- **Choose One:** Pick one type of yarn (a smooth, light-colored worsted weight is great for beginners) and one corresponding hook or needle size. Don't worry about anything else.
- **Learn a Single Stitch:** Master the knit stitch or the single crochet stitch. That's it. You can make countless beautiful things with just one stitch.
- **Start Small:** Your first project should be small and achievable. Think a dishcloth, a coaster, or just a simple square.
- **Practice in Short Bursts:** Set a timer for 20 minutes a day. The goal is to build a consistent, low-pressure ritual, not to finish a project quickly.
- **Set Honest Expectations:** Your first few attempts will likely be uneven and imperfect. That is part of the process. Every expert was once a beginner.

Joy-First Project Ideas

Choose a project that matches your energy level, not one that feels like a burden.

- **Micro-Projects (for a quick win):** A single granny square, a simple dishcloth, or a set of coasters.
- **Medium-Sized Projects (for a bit more focus):** A chunky beanie, a simple garter-stitch scarf, or a sweet baby hat.
- **Low-Energy Comfort Stitching:** On days when you feel drained, don't worry about a project at all. Just knit back and forth on a rectangle or crochet a single, large granny square.
- **Higher-Energy Projects (when you're feeling ambitious):** A cozy lap blanket made of simple squares or a beginner-friendly shawl.

Make It Cozy and Consistent

Turn your crafting time into a true sanctuary.

- **Create a Stitch Corner:** Designate a comfy chair with good lighting. Keep your project, a small pair of scissors, and your hook or needles in a dedicated basket.

- **Pair It with Pleasure:** Make a cup of tea, put on a favorite playlist or podcast, and put your phone on "Do Not Disturb."
- **Keep a Stitch Journal:** Snap a quick photo of your progress each time you sit down to work. It's incredibly motivating to look back and see how far you've come.

Community, Generosity, and Troubleshooting

Crafting doesn't have to be a solo activity.

- **Find Your People:** Visit a local yarn store for classes, join a friendly online crafting group, or start a stitch circle with friends.
- **Stitch for Charity:** Many organizations collect handmade hats, blankets, and shawls for those in need. Crafting with a purpose can be deeply fulfilling.
- **Embrace Frogging:** Ripping out stitches (called "frogging" because you "rip-it, rip-it") isn't failure; it's learning. Every stitcher does it.
- **Take Care of Your Hands:** Take frequent breaks to stretch your hands, wrists, and shoulders.
- **Adopt a Perfection-Free Motto:** The goal is a handmade item, not a machine-made one. The little imperfections are what give it character and heart.

Knitting and crocheting are more than just hobbies; they are practices of mindfulness, creativity, and self-compassion. They teach us that with a little patience, we can create something beautiful.

Shift 38

- Storytelling and Creativity

- M.G. plays with words and finds adventure in familiar places, turning chaos into creativity.

I love this part because I am a storyteller...

Why Storytelling Lifts Your Spirit

We are all natural-born storytellers. It's how our brains make sense of the world, especially during times of stress. When life feels chaotic, imposing a narrative structure; a beginning, a middle, and an end - gives us a sense of order and control. This act of "sense-making" helps us process difficult emotions and find meaning in our experiences.

Storytelling gives us the power to reframe our circumstances. A frustrating traffic jam can become a "period of forced stillness," and a mistake can be reframed as an unexpected plot twist. This creates cognitive distance, allowing us to step back from our immediate feelings and observe them with more curiosity and less judgment. It grants us agency. We may not be able to control what happens to us, but we can always choose the story we tell about it. By finding humor, awe, or adventure in the everyday, we embark on micro-adventures that cost nothing but a little imagination.

Wordplay as Mood Play

The words you choose have power. Playing with language is a simple way to inject creativity and lightness into your day. You don't have to be a poet; just get curious.

- **Metaphor:** What if your anxiety isn't a monster, but a "fog that will eventually lift"? What if your fatigue is a "heavy blanket" you can choose to set aside for a few minutes?
- **Alliteration:** Describe your walk as a "serene Sunday stroll." Notice the "babbling brook" or the "chattering children." The musicality of language is inherently pleasing.
- **Unlikely Comparisons:** This pile of laundry is "Mount Fold-more." A little humor can deflate dread.

Story Prompts for Familiar Places

You don't need to go far to find a good story. Your next adventure is waiting in the most familiar places.

- **The Kitchen Quest:** What epic meal are you preparing? What rare ingredients (spices from the back of the cabinet) will you use?

- **The Laundry Odyssey:** You are a brave explorer navigating the treacherous seas of sorted colors, seeking the lost land of matching socks.
- **Bus-Stop Cast of Characters:** Give the strangers around you secret identities. That woman is a retired spy; that man is a time traveler.
- **Desk-Drawer Time Capsule:** What story do the objects in your desk drawer tell? The old pen, the single paperclip, the forgotten photo.
- **The Neighborhood Myth:** Create a legend about your street. Why does that one tree lean just so? What secret is hidden beneath that loose paving stone?

Turning Chaos into Creativity

When things feel messy, use these practices to shape the chaos into a story.

- **Name the Chapter:** What is the title of the chapter of your life you are in right now? "The Great Unlearning"? "Finding My Footing"? "An Unexpected Interlude"?
- **Worst-Then-Best Line:** Describe your day in the worst possible way. Then, rewrite the same events using the most positive, heroic language you can muster.

- **10-Minute Fairy Tale:** Rewrite your day as a fairy tale, complete with a hero (you), a challenge, and a magical helper (a kind word, a good song).
- **Soundtrack a Scene:** If this moment of your life were in a movie, what song would be playing? I do that with my books. Each book has a soundtrack.
- **Object Monologue:** Pick an object in your room and imagine what it would say if it could talk. What has it witnessed? This is so much fun!

How to Share Your Story (or Keep It for Yourself)

- **Voice Note to Self:** Record a short, 1-minute summary of your day as a story.
- **Tiny Text:** Send a friend a one-sentence story: "Today, I battled the dragon of procrastination and won a small victory."
- **100-Word Micro-Story:** Write a tiny story about your day. The constraint makes it a fun, low-pressure game.
- **Bedtime Story:** As you fall asleep, tell yourself a calming story about your day, focusing on one good thing that happened.

The stories we tell ourselves are the houses we live in. By choosing our words with intention and our plots with imagination, we can build a home inside ourselves that is resilient and hopeful.

Shift 39

- Tailored Approach

- M.L. advises adapting strategies depending on the cause of sadness and including the right support system for healing.

When you're feeling sad, it's common to hear well-meaning advice: "Get outside!" "Talk to a friend!" "Just be positive!" While these suggestions come from a good place, they often miss a crucial point: what soothes one person can feel like a burden to another.

There is no one-size-fits-all remedy for sadness. The strategies that truly help are as unique as we are. Recognizing this is the first step toward finding a path to healing that feels authentic and effective for you.

Why One Size Doesn't Fit All

What works for you on any given day depends on many factors. The cause of your sadness matters immensely. The deep ache of grief from a loss requires a different approach than the flat, exhausted feeling of burnout. Disappointment over a setback needs a different response than the gnawing emptiness of loneliness.

Your own temperament plays a huge role. An introvert might find solace in quiet reflection, while an extravert may need to connect with people to recharge. Your sensory needs, cultural background, faith, and personal history all shape what feels comforting. Gender socialization can also influence our coping styles; for example, some men might feel more comfortable connecting through a shared activity rather than a face-to-face talk, while some women might find verbal processing more natural. The key is to move beyond stereotypes and honor what genuinely works for you, regardless of expectations.

A Menu of Strategies for Different Kinds of Sadness

Your approach should match the situation. Here are a few examples of how you might tailor your response.

When you're grieving an acute loss:

- **Strategies:** Allow yourself to feel without judgment. Create a small ritual to honor what was lost. Seek comfort in quiet, trusted company. Look at old photos or listen to meaningful music.
- **Use with Care:** Avoid pressure to "move on" quickly. Be cautious with large social gatherings that might feel overwhelming.

When you're overwhelmed by stress or burnout:

- **Strategies:** Prioritize rest, even if it's just a 10-minute break with your eyes closed. Drastically lower your expectations for the day. Say "no" to one small thing. Do a simple, repetitive activity like washing dishes or folding laundry to calm your mind.
- **Use with Care:** High-intensity exercise might add more stress; a gentle walk is often better. Avoid trying to "power through" with caffeine, which may increase anxiety.

When you feel lonely or socially isolated:

- **Strategies:** Send a low-pressure text to a friend. Visit a coffee shop or library just to be around the quiet hum of other people. Listen to a podcast with a warm, friendly host. Cuddle with a pet.
- **Use with Care:** Forcing yourself to go to a loud party might make you feel more isolated. Be wary of social media, which can sometimes amplify feelings of being left out.

When you're disappointed or feeling like a failure:

- **Strategies:** Talk to a friend who you know will remind you of your strengths. Write down a list of past challenges you have overcome.

Engage in a hobby you feel competent at, even if it's small.

- **Use with Care:** Avoid comparing yourself to others. Be mindful of internal self-criticism; try to speak to yourself as you would a dear friend.

Build Your Own Personal Support Plan

Instead of searching for a single magic bullet, create a personal toolkit with a few reliable options. Think of it as a small, curated menu you can choose from depending on your energy and needs. Aim to have at least one idea for each of these categories:

1. **An Anchor Practice (for grounding):** Something to calm your nervous system.
   - *Examples: Deep breathing, holding a warm mug, listening to a grounding piece of music, stepping outside for five minutes.*
2. **A Mood-Lifting Practice (for activation):** A small act of pleasure or accomplishment.
   - *Examples: Watching a funny video, listening to an upbeat song, completing one tiny task, eating a favorite snack.*
3. **A Connection Practice (for support):** A way to feel less alone.
   - *Examples: Texting a friend, calling a family member, praying or meditating, spending time with a pet.*

4. **A Restorative Practice (for recovery):** An action that replenishes your energy.
   - *Examples: Taking a nap, drinking a glass of water, eating a nourishing meal, going to bed early.*

Your Support System Map

Healing doesn't happen in a vacuum. It's helpful to know who to turn to for different kinds of support.

- **Your Inner Circle:** These are the 1-3 people you can be completely honest with. They offer emotional support without judgment.
- **Your Practical Helpers:** These are people who can help with concrete tasks when you're low on energy, like picking up groceries or watching your kids.
- **Your Professional Supports:** This includes therapists, doctors, or spiritual leaders who provide expert guidance.

It's okay to ask for what you need. A simple, "I'm having a hard day, could you just listen for a few minutes?" or "I'm feeling overwhelmed, would you be able to help me with this task?" can make all the difference.

Shift 40

- Affirmations

- Using positive affirmations can help shift the focus away from sadness and towards positivity.

Why Affirmations Can Help

Using positive affirmations is a way to consciously choose the direction of your thoughts. Our brains are wired to pay attention to threats (the negativity bias). Affirmations work by intentionally creating a new, more positive track.

Through repetition, you can leverage neuroplasticity; your brain's ability to form new neural pathways. The more you repeat a thought, the stronger that pathway becomes, making the thought more automatic over time. Affirmations act as state-dependent reminders; when you practice a calming phrase while you are calm, it becomes easier to recall that phrase and its associated feeling when you start to feel stressed.

Pairing these words with a physical action, like deep breathing or placing a hand on your heart, strengthens the mind-body connection and makes the practice even more effective.

How to Craft an Affirmation That Works for You

For an affirmation to be effective, it has to feel believable to your nervous system. Grand statements like "I am a millionaire" when you're struggling with finances can create internal conflict. The key is to make them compassionate and rooted in the present.

- **Use the Present Tense:** Phrase it as if it's already true. "I am learning" instead of "I will learn."
- **Make it Believable:** If "I love my body" feels like a stretch, try "I am learning to appreciate my body for what it can do."
- **Be Specific to Your Situation:** Tailor the phrase to what you need most right now.
- **Focus on Your Values:** Connect the affirmation to what is truly important to you, like peace, resilience, or kindness.

Here are some examples of reframing negative self-talk:

- Instead of: "I'm failing." Try: "I am learning and growing through this."
- Instead of: "I'm so overwhelmed." Try: "I can handle this one step at a time."
- Instead of: "I shouldn't feel this way." Try: "I can be gentle with myself as I feel this."

Affirmations are not about pretending everything is perfect. They are about choosing to water the seeds of hope, resilience, and peace within you.

They are a quiet, powerful way to guide your mind back home to a place of strength and self-compassion.

Shift 41

- Goal-Setting and Taking Action

- Setting achievable goals and taking action towards them can give a sense of purpose and motivation to overcome sadness.

Why Taking Action Lifts Your Mood

When we feel sad or stuck, our world can feel like it's shrinking. Setting a small, achievable goal and taking action toward it is a powerful way to push back. This process works on several levels to improve our mood. First, it restores a sense of agency; the feeling that you have control over your actions and can influence your life. This is a direct antidote to the helplessness that often accompanies sadness.

Taking a step, no matter how small, provides a sense of direction and purpose. It moves you from a passive state to an active one, a principle known as "behavioral activation." Often, motivation doesn't come first; action does. As you make progress, your brain releases dopamine, a neurotransmitter associated with reward and motivation, creating a positive feedback loop. Each tiny win builds on the last, gradually shifting your identity from someone who is "stuck" to someone who is "capable."

How to Set Goals When Your Energy is Low

The key to goal-setting during a tough time is to make the goals ridiculously small. The objective is not to be productive but to create forward momentum.

- Go MICRO: Think smaller than small. Not "clean the kitchen," but "put one dish in the sink." Not "go for a run," but "put on your walking shoes."
- Narrow Your Scope: Focus on just one thing for the next hour.
- Use Time-Boxing: Set a timer for just five or ten minutes and work on one thing until it goes off.
- Embrace Minimum Viable Effort: Ask yourself, "What is the absolute smallest amount of effort I can put toward this?"
- Choose Just One Next Step: Don't map out the whole journey. Just identify the very next physical action.
- Create "If-Then" Plans: Make a simple plan, like "If I finish my tea, then I will rinse out the mug."

Create Action Loops and Celebrate

Progress isn't a straight line; it's a loop.

- Plan: Choose your tiny action.
- Do: Take the step.

- Reflect: Acknowledge that you did it. Say to yourself, "I did that." This part is crucial. It's how your brain registers the win.
- Adjust: Based on how it felt, decide what your next tiny step will be.

It's vital to celebrate these micro-wins. A mental high-five or a quiet "good job" reinforces the positive behavior.

Navigating Obstacles

Your own mind can be the biggest hurdle. Be on the lookout for these common traps:

- Perfectionism: The goal is not to do it perfectly, but to do it at all. Done is better than perfect.
- All-or-Nothing Thinking: If you can't do a full workout, a five-minute walk still counts. If you can't clean the whole house, tidying one surface is a victory.
- Decision Fatigue: When choosing feels too hard, just pick the easiest or closest option.

Use compassionate self-talk. If you miss a goal, don't scold yourself. Just say, "That was tough. Let's try an even smaller step tomorrow."

Taking action is not about erasing sadness. It's about reminding yourself that you are still the driver of your life. You can still choose your direction, one small and courageous step at a time.

OVERCOMING

A Final Word of Encouragement

Navigating sadness isn't about finding a single magic cure, but about gently building a personal toolkit of practices that bring light, one small action at a time. The journey begins with giving yourself permission to feel what you feel, without judgment. From there, it's about choosing small, intentional steps that ground you in the present and reconnect you with yourself, with others, and with hope. As we've explored, this can be as simple as changing the song you're singing, stepping outside for a short walk, or choosing to focus on a single, comforting verse or phrase.

The strategies that work are the ones that feel authentic to you. For some, the rhythmic motion of knitting or crocheting can quiet a busy mind, while for others, reframing the day as a story brings a sense of agency and play. The key is to create a personal menu of options; a grounding practice, a mood-lifting one, a way to connect, and a method to restore your energy. We've seen how tiny goals, like putting one dish in the sink, can create powerful forward momentum, and how a simple gratitude practice can train our brains to spot the good that still exists, even on hard days.

Ultimately, this is a practice of compassion. It's about recognizing what you need in the moment. Remember that you are the expert on your own heart.

More Ways to Find Your Footing

Here are some additional practices to help you navigate and lift the low moments:

- **Hydrate Well:** Drink a large glass of water. Dehydration can significantly impact mood and energy levels.
- **Watch Something Funny:** Find a favorite comedian, a funny animal video, or a lighthearted sitcom to watch for a short mood boost.
- **Plan Something Small to Look Forward To:** It could be a favorite meal tomorrow, a call with a friend this weekend, or watching a new movie release.
- **Care for Something Living:** Water a plant or feed a bird. Focusing on another living thing can shift your perspective.
- **Engage in "Bilateral Stimulation":** While seated, gently tap your hands on your knees, alternating left, right, left, right, for a minute to help calm your nervous system.
- **Do One Kind Thing for Your Future Self:** Lay out your clothes for tomorrow, make a simple

lunch, or put your keys where you'll easily find them.

- **Stretch Your Body:** Gently stretch your neck, shoulders, and back for a few minutes to release physical tension.
- **Give a Hug:** If you have a trusted person or pet nearby, a warm hug can release oxytocin and promote feelings of connection and safety.

Finding what helps you navigate sadness is a process of gentle experimentation. Be curious. Be compassionate. What worked yesterday might not work today, and that's perfectly okay. Give yourself permission to try, to let go of what doesn't serve you, and to lean on what does. You are the foremost expert on your own heart. Trust its wisdom as you find your way back to the light.

On the pages that follow, you'll find tips and actions to inspire you. These include affirmations, songs, and simple recipes to help you navigate and lift those low moments.

THE MOOD SHIFT PLAN

A Curated List of Affirmations and Mantras

Find a few that resonate with you.

For Grounding and Soothing:

- I am safe and supported in this moment.
- I am doing enough. I am enough.
- This feeling is temporary and it will pass.
- I can find calm, even in the middle of a storm.

For Hope and Mood-Lifting:

- I am open to seeing the good in this day.
- Joy is available to me.
- My capacity for happiness is greater than my sadness.
- Something good is waiting for me.

For Action and Agency:

- I have the strength to take the next small step.
- I am capable of handling challenges with grace.
- I am the author of my own story.
- My actions create momentum.

Faith-Forward Options:

- God's peace is guarding my heart and mind.
- I can do all things through Christ who gives me strength.
- I am held in a love that never fails.
- The joy of the Lord is my strength.

How to Remember to Use Them

The best affirmation is the one you remember to use.

- **Habit-Stacking:** Say your affirmation while you brush your teeth or wait for coffee to brew.
- **Visual Cues:** Write it on a sticky note and put it on your mirror, laptop, or dashboard. Make it your phone's lock screen.
- **Set Alarms:** Set a few alarms on your phone with the affirmation as the label.
- **Audio Recordings:** Record yourself saying the phrases and listen to them on your commute.
- **Physical Anchors:** Wear a specific ring or bracelet. Every time you notice it, let it be a reminder to repeat your phrase.
- **Environment Labels:** Place a sticky note that says "peace" on your desk or "nourish" on your fridge.

Your 7-Day Affirmation Challenge

I invite you to experiment with this practice for one week.

- **Day 1:** Choose one affirmation from the list that resonates with you.
- **Day 2:** Write it down and place it where you will see it often.
- **Day 3:** Set a phone alarm to remind you to say it in the middle of the day.
- **Day 4:** Try pairing your affirmation with three deep breaths.
- **Day 5:** Reframe one negative thought you have with a more compassionate phrase.
- **Day 6:** Record yourself saying your affirmation and listen to it once.
- **Day 7:** Notice how it feels. Has repeating this phrase shifted anything for you?

One-Week "Give Back, Feel Better" Mini-Plan

- **Day 1:** Brainstorm two or three causes you care about.
- **Day 3:** Research one local organization tied to one of those causes.
- **Day 5:** Send one inquiry email or sign up for an online newsletter.
- **Day 7:** Complete one micro-volunteering act, like writing a positive review.

Journaling 101

Here is a simple, seven-day prompt series. Aim for just 5-10 minutes each day.

- **Day 1:** What is one thing, big or small, that is weighing on my mind right now? Describe it without judgment.
- **Day 2:** Write about a simple moment of joy you experienced recently. Use all five senses to describe it.
- **Day 3:** If I could give my younger self one piece of advice, what would it be and why?
- **Day 4:** List three things you are good at. They don't have to be grand talents; maybe you make a great cup of tea or are a patient listener.
- **Day 5:** Write a letter to an emotion you're feeling (e.g., "Dear Anxiety," or "Dear Hope,"). What do you want to say to it?
- **Day 6:** What is a place; real or imagined - where you feel completely at peace? Describe it in detail.
- **Day 7:** Looking back on this week, what is one thing I learned or one small victory I can celebrate?

Your 7-Day Audio Uplift Plan

I invite you to try weaving some positive audio into your week.

- **Day 1:** Listen to one 15-minute TED Talk while you drink your morning beverage.
- **Day 2:** Play an uplifting music playlist while you get ready.
- **Day 3:** Find a 20-minute podcast episode to listen to on a walk or commute.
- **Day 4:** Share a favorite episode or talk with a friend.
- **Day 5:** Listen in silence. Take a break and notice the sounds around you.
- **Day 6:** Try a new-to-you genre of podcast.
- **Day 7:** Choose an audiobook to start from your local library's free app.

A 7-Day Reading Reset

I invite you to rediscover the joy of reading.

- **Day 1:** Visit your local library or browse its app. Place a hold on one book that sounds interesting.
- **Day 2:** Create a cozy reading spot in your home.
- **Day 3:** Read for 15 minutes with your phone in another room.
- **Day 4:** Try an audiobook sample while you do chores or go for a walk.
- **Day 5:** Read the first chapter of a new book. No pressure to continue if it doesn't hook you.
- **Day 6:** Talk to a friend about a book you both have read and loved.
- **Day 7:** Spend 30 minutes reading before bed instead of looking at a screen.

Your 7-Day Gratitude Challenge

I invite you to try this simple practice for one week and notice how it feels.

- **Day 1:** Write down three good things that happened today.
- **Day 2:** Send a thank-you text to a friend.
- **Day 3:** Take a 10-minute gratitude walk.
- **Day 4:** Before one meal, pause and think of one reason you're grateful for it.
- **Day 5:** Give someone a specific, genuine compliment.
- **Day 6:** Create a three-song gratitude playlist.
- **Day 7:** Before you go to sleep, recall one happy moment from your day.

Your "Clear Space, Clear Mind" 5-Day Mini-Plan

I invite you to try a few small acts of organization.

- **Day 1:** Set a timer for 10 minutes and clear your kitchen counters.
- **Day 2:** Tidy your nightstand before you get into bed.
- **Day 3:** Apply the two-minute rule all day.
- **Day 4:** Sort through the mail or any paper pile in your entryway.
- **Day 5:** Perform a five-minute "closing ritual" at your desk before you finish work.

Clearing your physical space creates mental space. It's a quiet, powerful way to tell yourself that you are worthy of a calm and supportive environment, starting right where you are.

Your 7-Day "Story Spark" Mini-Plan

I invite you to play with the stories you tell yourself.

- **Day 1:** Narrate one simple task as a grand adventure.
- **Day 2:** Give a secret identity to a stranger you see - I love doing this. I create so many nicknames - it makes me smile.
- **Day 3:** Name the chapter you're in right now.
- **Day 4:** Send a friend a one-sentence story about your day.
- **Day 5:** Describe a feeling you have using a creative metaphor.
- **Day 6:** Soundtrack one moment of your day. What song is playing?
- **Day 7:** Tell yourself a one-minute bedtime story about something good that happened.

Your 7-Day "Stitch for Calm" Mini-Plan

I invite you to try this gentle introduction to yarn crafting and see how it feels.

- **Day 1:** Visit a craft store and buy one skein of yarn and one hook or needle.
- **Day 2:** Watch a video tutorial and practice a single stitch for 15 minutes.
- **Day 3:** Set up a cozy stitch corner in your home.
- **Day 4:** Practice your stitch for 20 minutes while listening to music.
- **Day 5:** Start a simple project, like a dishcloth or scarf.
- **Day 6:** Take a photo of your progress. Notice how much you've made!
- **Day 7:** Stitch for 15 minutes and notice the calming rhythm of the craft.

Praise on Purpose: 31 Days to a Stronger Spirit

As a person of faith, here is a 31 day plan that I used for Praise and Worship. If you are of the Christian faith, I hope you find it hopeful. On the harder days I sing songs like - Way Maker, Raise a Hallelujah, and Break Every Chain. For full effect, move your body as you sing the song. Also, try to smile for at least 10 seconds as you sing.

If you are of a different faith, you may substitute with songs that calm you.

Day 1: *Way Maker - Sinach*

- Why: Repetitive chorus anchors trust in hard seasons.
- Mantra: "You are here. I worship You."
- Sing it: Hum the chorus first, then sing quietly, then full voice.

Day 2: *You Will Win - Jekalyn Carr*

- Why: Victory declarations counter negative self-talk.
- Mantra: "I am built to win."
- Sing it: Speak the chorus as affirmations, then sing them.

Day 3: *Graves into Gardens - Elevation Worship*

- Why: Reframes loss into renewal.
- Mantra: "Mourning to dancing."
- Sing it: Clap on the chorus

Day 4: *The Blessing - Kari Jobe & Cody Carnes*

- Why: Sung benediction calms the nervous system.
- Mantra: "May His peace be upon me."
- Sing it: Slow breaths; imagine the blessings.

Day 5: *Raise a Hallelujah - Bethel Music*

- Why: Courage in the storm builds resilience.
- Mantra: "My song is a weapon."
- Sing it: Alternate you/crowd; call-and-response style.

Day 6: *I Smile - Kirk Franklin*

- Why: Chooses joy without denying pain.
- Mantra: "I choose joy today."
- Sing it: Add a gentle sway; smile as you sing.

Day 7: *Goodness of God - Bethel Music*

- Why: Gratitude redirects attention to hope.
- Mantra: "Your goodness is running after me."
- Sing it: List three gratitudes between choruses.

Day 8: *Jireh - Elevation & Maverick City*

- Why: "I'm already loved" dissolves scarcity.
- Mantra: "I am enough."
- Sing it: Emphasize "enough"; hand on heart.

Day 9: *Oceans (Where Feet May Fail) - Hillsong UNITED*

- Why: Courage to step into the unknown.
- Mantra: "Spirit, lead me."
- Sing it: Stretch the long notes for grounding.

Day 10: *Amazing Grace (My Chains Are Gone) - Chris Tomlin*

- Why: Release and renewal.
- Mantra: "My chains are gone."
- Sing it: Exhale fully after "are gone."

Day 11: *Break Every Chain - Tasha Cobbs Leonard*

- Why: Powerful decree to break heaviness.
- Mantra: "There is power in His name."
- Sing it: Stomp or clap to embody release.

Day 12: *This Year (Blessing) - Victor Thompson*

- Why: Future-focused blessing fuels hope.
- Mantra: "This year, I flourish."
- Sing it: Speak the refrain over your calendar, then sing.

Day 13: *Promises - Maverick City Music*

- Why: Faithfulness through changing seasons.
- Mantra: "Great is Your faithfulness."
- Sing it: Start with a whisper; build to a belt.

Day 14: *Not Afraid - Jesus Culture*

- Why: Names fear, chooses trust.
- Mantra: "I will not fear."
- Sing it: Lean on downbeats; steady your tempo.

Day 15: *Joyful - Dante Bowe*

- Why: Upbeat groove triggers movement.
- Mantra: "Joy is my strength."
- Sing it: March in place; sing the hook.

Day 16: *I Thank God - Maverick City Music x UPPERROOM*

- Why: Testimony-style gratitude boosts mood.
- Mantra: "You picked me up."
- Sing it: Say the testimony line; sing the chorus.

Day 17: *Brighter Day - Kirk Franklin*

- Why: Energetic optimism shifts state fast.
- Mantra: "It's a brighter day."
- Sing it: Snap or clap; emphasize syncopation.

Day 18: *Good Grace - Hillsong UNITED*

- Why: Collective hope, simple refrain.
- Mantra: "Let the praise go up."
- Sing it: Breathe in "praise," exhale "go up."

Day 19: *Blessings on Blessings - Anthony Brown*

- Why: Counts big and small wins.
- Mantra: "Blessings on blessings."
- Sing it: Finger count three blessings, then sing.

Day 20: *Miracle Worker - JJ Hairston*

- Why: Expectancy combats despair.
- Mantra: "You are a miracle worker."
- Sing it: Emphasize "are" to cement belief.

Day 21: *Fighting For Me - Riley Clemmons*

- Why: Reminds you you're not alone.
- Mantra: "You fight for me."
- Sing it: Soft verse; strong chorus.

Day 22: *Joy In The Morning - Tauren Wells*

- Why: Time-bound hope after night.
- Mantra: "Joy comes in the morning."
- Sing it: Morning routine - sing while making breakfast.

Day 23: *Speak The Name - Koryn Hawthorne*

- Why: Naming peace under pressure.
- Mantra: "Peace when I speak the Name."

- Sing it: Whisper the verse; sing the hook.

Day 24: *Never Lost - CeCe Winans*

- Why: Track record of victories.
- Mantra: "You never lost a battle."
- Sing it: Stand tall; open chest on chorus.

Day 25: *Firm Foundation (He Won't) - Cody Carnes*

- Why: Stability when emotions swing.
- Mantra: "He won't."
- Sing it: Tap your sternum lightly to feel resonance.

Day 26: *Take the Shackles Off My Feet - Mary Mary*

- Why: Permission to be loud and free.
- Mantra: "Make a joyful noise."
- Sing it: Volume up; release perfection.

Day 27: *Never Would Have Made It - Marvin Sapp*

- Why: Testimony = perspective shift.
- Mantra: "I made it."
- Sing it: Replace "I" with your name once.

Day 28: *See A Victory - Elevation Worship*

- Why: "The battle belongs" reduces burden.
- Mantra: "You turn it for good."
- Sing it: Visualize a challenge.

Day 29: *Joyful Joyful - Casting Crowns*

- Why: Classic exuberance lifts spirits.
- Mantra: "Hearts unfold like flowers."
- Sing it: Enunciate; smile as you sing.

Day 30: *Count Me In - Switch*

- Why: Recommitment to hope.
- Mantra: "Count me in."
- Sing it: Point to yourself on "me."

Day 31: *I'll Give Thanks - Housefires*

- Why: Gratitude seals the journey.
- Mantra: "I'll give thanks."
- Sing it: Journal one line you're thankful for, then sing.

Your One-Week Fresh Perspective Challenge

Here are seven simple prompts for the week ahead.

- **Day 1:** Drink your morning coffee or tea in a different spot than usual.
- **Day 2:** Listen to a 10-minute podcast on a topic you know nothing about.
- **Day 3:** Take a different route to or from work, the store, or on your daily walk.
- **Day 4:** Find and watch a short travel video of a place you've never seen.
- **Day 5:** Look up the history of a landmark in your own town.
- **Day 6:** Write down three beautiful things you notice on your way somewhere.
- **Day 7:** Rearrange one small thing in your living space, like a few books or a chair.

A Curated Bookshelf for Every Mood

Whether you need a warm hug in book form or a story so gripping you can't put it down, there's a book for you.

For a Feel-Good Escape

These books are comforting, gentle, and full of heart.

- *The House in the Cerulean Sea* by T.J. Klune
- *Evvie Drake Starts Over* by Linda Holmes
- *A Man Called Ove* by Fredrik Backman
- *The Guernsey Literary and Potato Peel Pie Society* by Mary Ann Shaffer and Annie Barrows
- *The House in the Cerulean Sea by* TJ Klune
- *Before I Let Go by* Kennedy Ryan
- *Honey Girl by* Morgan Rogers
- *Me Before You* by Jojo Moyes
- *Eleanor Oliphant Is Completely Fine* by Gail Honeyman
- *Red, White & Royal Blue* by Casey McQuiston
- *Royal Holiday by* Jasmine Guillory
- *Black Cake by* Charmaine Wilkerson
- *The Thursday Murder Club* by Richard Osman
- *Where the Crawdads Sing* by Delia Owens
- *Lessons in Chemistry* by Bonnie Garmus

- *Remarkably Bright Creatures* by Shelby Van Pelt

For Total Immersion (Unputdownable Plots)

When you need to be completely transported, these page-turners will grab you from the first chapter and not let go.

- *The Silent Patient* by Alex Michaelides
- *Gone Girl* by Gillian Flynn
- *Circe* by Madeline Miller
- *Razorblade Tears* by S. A. Cosby
- *The Fifth Season* by N. K. Jemisin
- *The Seven Husbands of Evelyn Hugo* by Taylor Jenkins Reid
- *Project Hail Mary* by Andy Weir
- *The Hunger Games* by Suzanne Collins
- *Fourth Wing* by Rebecca Yarros
- *All the Light We Cannot See* by Anthony Doerr
- *Big Little Lies* by Liane Moriarty
- *The Midnight Library* by Matt Haig
- *Verity* by Colleen Hoover
- *The City We Became* by N. K. Jemisin
- *The Inheritance of Orquídea Divina* by Zoraida Córdova

31 Simple Joy Recipes

Check out some recipes to take you through the hard days:

Classic Chocolate Chip Cookies

- Yield: About 24 cookies | Active: 15 min | Total: 30–35 min
- Ingredients:
    1. 2 1/4 cups all-purpose flour
    2. 1 cup granulated sugar
    3. 1/2 cup light brown sugar, packed
    4. 1 cup (2 sticks) unsalted butter, softened
    5. 2 large eggs
    6. 2 tsp vanilla extract
    7. 1 tsp baking soda
    8. 1/2 tsp fine salt
    9. 1 1/2 cups semi-sweet chocolate chips
- Method:
    1. Heat oven to 350°F (175°C). Line 2 baking sheets.
    2. Cream butter, granulated sugar, and brown sugar until fluffy (2–3 min). Beat in eggs and vanilla.
    3. Whisk flour, baking soda, and salt; fold into a wet mix. Stir in chips.

4. Scoop 1-tbsp mounds, spaced 2 inches apart; bake 9–11 min until edges are golden. Cool 5 min on sheet, then rack.

Simple Jollof Rice

- Yield: 6 servings | Active: 20 min | Total: 45–55 min
- Ingredients:
  1. 2 cups long-grain rice, rinsed
  2. 1/4 cup vegetable oil
  3. 1 large onion, chopped or blended
  4. 1 can (14–15 oz) tomato sauce OR blended 2 tomatoes + 1 red bell pepper + 1/2 onion
  5. 1–2 tbsp tomato paste
  6. 2 cups chicken or vegetable stock (plus more as needed)
  7. 1 tsp curry powder
  8. 1 tsp dried thyme
  9. 1 bay leaf
  10. 1/2–1 tsp salt, 1/2 tsp black pepper (to taste)
- Method:
  1. Heat oil; sauté the onion 3-4 min. Add tomato paste; cook for 3 min.
  2. Stir in tomato sauce/blend, curry, thyme, bay leaf; simmer 5-7 min until rich.
  3. Add stock, salt, pepper; stir. Cover tightly; cook high for 2mins.

4. Add rice; stir. Cover tightly; cook low
   25-30 min, stirring once and adding
   splashes of stock if needed.

Homemade Vanilla Ice Cream

- Yield: 1.5 quarts | Active: 10 min | Freeze: 6 hours
- Ingredients:
  1. 2 cups heavy whipping cream, cold
  2. 1 can (14 oz) sweetened condensed milk
  3. 2 tsp vanilla extract
  4. Optional mix-ins: 1 cup crushed cookies, chopped fruit, or chocolate chunks
- Method:
  1. Whip cream to stiff peaks (2–3 min).
  2. In a bowl, combine condensed milk and vanilla. Fold in whipped cream gently.
  3. Stir in mix-ins. Pour into loaf pan; cover and freeze for 6 hours or overnight.

Easy Puff Puff (Bofrot)

- Yield: 24–30 puffs | Active: 20 min | Rise: 45–60 min | Fry: 15 min
- Ingredients:
  1. 3 cups all-purpose flour
  2. 1/2 cup granulated sugar
  3. 2 tsp instant yeast
  4. 1/2 tsp salt
  5. 1/2 tsp ground nutmeg
  6. 2–2 1/4 cups warm water (as needed for thick batter)
  7. Neutral oil, for frying
- Method:
  1. Whisk dry ingredients. Add warm water gradually to form a thick, sticky batter.
  2. Cover; rise in a warm spot 45–60 min until doubled.
  3. Heat oil to 350°F (175°C). Scoop batter by heaping tablespoons; fry 2–3 min per side until deep golden. Drain.

Simple Skillet Lasagna

- Yield: 4–6 servings | Active: 20 min | Total: 35–40 min
- Ingredients:
  1. 1 lb ground beef or turkey
  2. 3 cups marinara sauce
  3. 8–10 dry lasagna noodles, broken into large pieces
  4. 1 cup water or broth (plus more as needed)
  5. 1 cup ricotta cheese
  6. 1 1/2 cups shredded mozzarella
  7. 1/4 cup grated Parmesan
  8. 1 tsp Italian seasoning, salt & pepper to taste
- Method:
  1. Brown meat in a large skillet; season. Stir in sauce and water; nestle in broken noodles.
  2. Cover; simmer low 15–18 min, stirring once or twice and adding a splash of water if dry, until noodles are tender.
  3. Dollop ricotta, sprinkle mozzarella and Parmesan; cover 2–3 min to melt.

Quick Peanut Brittle (Nkati-cake)

- Yield: About 1 lb | Active: 15 min | Total: 30 min (cooling included)
- Ingredients:
  1. 1 1/2 cup granulated sugar
  2. 1/4 cup water
  3. 1 1/2 cups roasted peanuts
  4. 2 tbsp unsalted butter
  5. 1/2 tsp vanilla extract (optional)
  6. Pinch of salt
- Method:
  1. Line a baking sheet; lightly butter it.
  2. In a saucepan, combine sugar, and water. Boil over medium, 5–6 min to light amber (300°F/149°C hard crack if using a thermometer).
  3. Stir in peanuts; cook 2–3 min until golden and fragrant. Remove from heat; quickly stir in butter, vanilla, and salt.
  4. Immediately pour thinly onto the sheet; tilt to spread. Cool 10–15 min; crack into pieces.

Caprese Salad

- Yield: 2–3 servings | Active: 10 min
- Ingredients:
    1. 2 large ripe tomatoes, sliced
    2. 8 oz fresh mozzarella, sliced
    3. 12–16 fresh basil leaves
    4. 2 tbsp extra-virgin olive oil
    5. 1–2 tsp balsamic glaze
    6. Pinch of salt & black pepper
- Method:
    1. Alternate tomato and mozzarella on a plate; tuck basil between.
    2. Drizzle olive oil and glaze; season lightly.

Sunshine Citrus Salad

- Yield: 2 servings | Active: 10 min
- Ingredients:
  1. 4 cups mixed greens
  2. 1 orange, segmented
  3. 1/2 avocado, sliced
  4. 2 tbsp thinly sliced red onion
  5. 2 tbsp vinaigrette (olive oil + lemon/orange juice + pinch salt)
- Method:
  1. Toss greens, orange, avocado, and onion gently.
  2. Dress just before serving.

Fluffy Scrambled Eggs

- Yield: 2 servings | Active: 8–10 min
- Ingredients:
    1. 4 large eggs
    2. 2 tbsp milk or cream
    3. 1 tbsp butter
    4. 1/4 tsp salt, pinch pepper
- Method:
    1. Whisk eggs, milk, salt, pepper.
    2. Melt butter on low heat; add eggs; stir slowly 4-6 min to soft curds.

One-Pot Tomato Soup

- Yield: 4 servings | Active: 10 min | Total: 25–30 min
- Ingredients:
  1. 1 tbsp olive oil
  2. 1 small onion, chopped
  3. 2 cloves garlic, minced
  4. 1 can (28 oz) crushed tomatoes
  5. 2 cups vegetable broth
  6. 1/4 cup cream (or milk), optional
  7. 1/2 tsp sugar, salt & pepper to taste
- Method:
  1. Sauté onion 3–4 min; add garlic 30 sec.
  2. Add tomatoes, broth, sugar; simmer for 15 min. Blend smooth (optional). Stir in cream; season.

Avocado Toast with Everything Spice

- Yield: 1 serving | Active: 5 min
- Ingredients:
  1. 1 thick slice hearty bread
  2. 1/2 ripe avocado
  3. 1 tsp lemon juice
  4. 1/2–1 tsp everything bagel seasoning
  5. Pinch of salt
- Method:
  1. Toast bread. Smash avocado with lemon juice and salt; spread.
  2. Sprinkle seasoning; serve.

Berry & Yogurt Parfait

- Yield: 2 servings | Active: 5–7 min
- Ingredients:
  1. 1 1/2 cups Greek yogurt
  2. 1 cup mixed berries (fresh or thawed)
  3. 1/2 cup granola
  4. 1–2 tsp honey
- Method:
  1. Layer yogurt, berries, granola; repeat.
  2. Drizzle honey on top.

Simple Fried Rice

- Yield: 3–4 servings | Active: 15 min
- Ingredients:
    1. 3 cups cooked rice
    2. 2 tbsp soy sauce (plus to taste)
    3. 2 eggs, beaten
    4. 1 cup frozen peas and carrots
    5. 2 tbsp oil (neutral or sesame blend)
    6. 1 tsp sesame oil (finish), optional
- Method:
    1. Scramble eggs in 1 tbsp oil; set aside.
    2. Stir-fry veg in 1 tbsp oil 2–3 min; add rice and soy, breaking clumps 3–4 min. Stir in eggs; finish with sesame oil.

Cinnamon Sugar Toast

- Yield: 1–2 servings | Active: 5 min
- Ingredients:
  1. 2 slices bread
  2. 1–2 tbsp softened butter
  3. 1 tbsp sugar
  4. 1/2 tsp cinnamon
- Method:
  1. Toast bread. Mix sugar + cinnamon.
  2. Butter toast; sprinkle cinnamon sugar generously.

Banana "Nice" Cream

- Yield: 2 servings | Active: 5 min
- Ingredients:
    1. 3 ripe bananas, sliced and frozen
    2. 2–3 tbsp milk of choice
    3. 1/2 tsp vanilla extract (optional)
- Method:
    1. Blend frozen banana with milk and vanilla until smooth.
    2. Serve soft or freeze 30–60 min for firmer scoops.

Easy Guacamole

- Yield: 2–3 servings | Active: 10 min
- Ingredients:
  1. 2 ripe avocados
  2. 1 tbsp lime juice
  3. 2 tbsp finely chopped red onion
  4. 1 tbsp chopped cilantro
  5. 1/4 tsp salt
- Method:
  1. Mash avocados; fold in lime, onion, cilantro, salt.
  2. Adjust seasoning; serve immediately.

Simple Lemonade

- Yield: 4 servings | Active: 10 min
- Ingredients:
    1. 1/2 cup fresh lemon juice (3–4 lemons)
    2. 4 cups cold water
    3. 1/3–1/2 cup sugar or honey (to taste)
- Method:
    1. Stir juice, water, and sweetener until dissolved.
    2. Add ice; serve.

Gooey Grilled Cheese

- Yield: 1 sandwich | Active: 8–10 min
- Ingredients:
  1. 2 slices bread
  2. 2–3 slices cheese (about 2–3 oz)
  3. 1 tbsp butter
- Method:
  1. Butter outsides of bread; sandwich cheese inside.
  2. Cook medium heat 3–4 min per side until golden and melty.

Sheet Pan Chicken & Veggies

- Yield: 4 servings | Active: 10 min | Total: 30–35 min
- Ingredients:
  1. 1.5 lbs chicken thighs or breasts, chunked
  2. 4 cups mixed veggies (broccoli, peppers, carrots)
  3. 2 tbsp olive oil
  4. 1 tsp dried Italian herbs
  5. 1/2 tsp salt, 1/4 tsp pepper
- Method:
  1. Toss all on a sheet pan; season and oil.
  2. Roast at 425°F (220°C) 22–28 min, stirring once.

Classic Hummus

- Yield: 2 cups | Active: 10 min
- Ingredients:
  1. 1 can (15 oz) chickpeas, drained (reserve liquid)
  2. 1/4 cup chickpea liquid or water
  3. 1/3 cup tahini
  4. 2 tbsp lemon juice
  5. 1 small garlic clove
  6. 2 tbsp olive oil
  7. 1/2 tsp salt
- Method:
  1. Blend all until very smooth, adding liquid to desired creaminess.
  2. Drizzle with olive oil to serve.

No-Bake Energy Bites

- Yield: 16–20 bites | Active: 10 min | Chill: 30 min
- Ingredients:
    1. 1 1/2 cups rolled oats
    2. 1/2 cup peanut butter
    3. 1/3 cup honey
    4. 1/3 cup chocolate chips or raisins
    5. Pinch of salt
- Method:
    1. Mix well; rest 5 min.
    2. Roll 1-tbsp balls; chill 30 min.

Italian Bruschetta

- Yield: 8–10 toasts | Active: 12–15 min
- Ingredients:
  1. 1 small baguette, sliced
  2. 2 cups diced ripe tomatoes
  3. 1 small garlic clove, minced (plus 1 whole clove to rub)
  4. 2 tbsp chopped basil
  5. 2 tbsp olive oil, plus more for brushing
  6. 1/4 tsp salt
- Method:
  1. Brush bread; toast 400°F (205°C) 6–8 min.
  2. Mix tomatoes, minced garlic, basil, oil, salt. Rub toasts with whole garlic; top with tomato mix.

Simple Dal

- Yield: 4 servings | Active: 10 min | Total: 25–30 min
- Ingredients:
  1. 1 cup red lentils, rinsed
  2. 4 cups water or broth
  3. 1/2 tsp turmeric
  4. 1 tsp grated ginger
  5. 1 small garlic clove, minced
  6. 1/2 tsp salt
- Method:
  1. Simmer lentils with water, turmeric, ginger, garlic 20–25 min until creamy.
  2. Salt to taste; finish with a drizzle of oil or ghee (optional).

Hot Chocolate from Scratch

- Yield: 2 cups | Active: 7–8 min
- Ingredients:
    1. 2 cups milk
    2. 2 tbsp cocoa powder
    3. 1-2 tbsp sugar
    4. Pinch cinnamon or chili powder
    5. Pinch salt
- Method:
    1. Warm milk; whisk in cocoa, sugar, spice, salt until steamy and smooth.

Greek Tzatziki

- Yield: 1 1/2 cups | Active: 10 min
- Ingredients:
    1. 1 cup Greek yogurt
    2. 1/2 cup grated cucumber, squeezed dry
    3. 1 tbsp lemon juice
    4. 1 tbsp chopped dill
    5. 1 small garlic clove, minced
    6. Pinch salt
- Method:
    1. Mix all; chill 15 min.

Simple Crepes

- Yield: 8–10 crepes | Active: 15 min | Rest: 10 min (optional)
- Ingredients:
    1. 1 cup all-purpose flour
    2. 2 large eggs
    3. 1 1/4 cups milk
    4. 1 tbsp melted butter
    5. Pinch salt
- Method:
    1. Whisk to a thin batter; rest 10 min.
    2. Lightly butter pan; pour 1/4 cup, swirl thin; cook 1 min, flip 20–30 sec.

Baked Apples with Cinnamon

- Yield: 4 apples | Active: 10 min | Total: 35–40 min
- Ingredients:
    1. 4 apples (e.g., Honeycrisp)
    2. 4 tbsp brown sugar
    3. 4 tbsp butter
    4. 1 tsp cinnamon
    5. Pinch salt
- Method:
    1. Core apples; fill each with 1 tbsp sugar, 1 tbsp butter, sprinkle cinnamon and salt.
    2. Bake 350°F (175°C) 25–30 min until tender.

Shakshuka for One

- Yield: 1 serving | Active: 15 min
- Ingredients:
  1. 1 tsp olive oil
  2. 1/4 small onion, chopped
  3. 1/2 cup canned crushed tomatoes
  4. Pinch cumin, pinch paprika
  5. 1 egg
  6. 1–2 tbsp crumbled feta
  7. Salt & pepper to taste
- Method:
  1. Sauté onion 2–3 min; add tomatoes and spices; simmer 5–6 min.
  2. Make a well; crack egg; cover 3–4 min to desired doneness. Top with feta.

Easy Cornbread Muffins

- Yield: 12 muffins | Active: 10 min | Bake: 15–18 min
- Ingredients:
  1. 1 cup cornmeal
  2. 1 cup all-purpose flour
  3. 1/3 cup sugar
  4. 1 tbsp baking powder
  5. 1/2 tsp salt
  6. 1 cup milk
  7. 1/3 cup oil
  8. 1 large egg
- Method:
  1. Heat oven to 400°F (205°C). Combine dry; whisk wet separately.
  2. Stir together just until moistened; fill tin 3/4 full; bake 15–18 min.

Mango Lassi

- Yield: 2 servings | Active: 5 min
- Ingredients:
  1. 1 1/2 cups ripe mango chunks
  2. 1 cup plain yogurt
  3. 1/4 cup milk
  4. 1–2 tsp honey (optional)
  5. Pinch cardamom
- Method:
  1. Blend until smooth and frothy; chill.

Garlic Bread

- Yield: 8–10 slices | Active: 10 min | Bake: 8–10 min
- Ingredients:
    1. 1 French loaf, sliced
    2. 1/2 cup softened butter
    3. 3 cloves garlic, minced
    4. 1 tsp dried parsley
    5. Pinch salt
- Method:
    1. Mix butter, garlic, parsley, salt; spread on slices.
    2. Bake 375°F (190°C) 8–10 min until fragrant and golden at edges.

A NOTE OF THANKS

Thanks for reading.

This book would not exist without the incredible community that formed around a simple online question about sadness.

Thank you for sharing your heartfelt wisdom: Natalie Thompson Oliver, Arialle Kennedy Smith, Azwimbavhi Nkoth, Dr. Julie Padgett Jones, Betsy Neely Sikma, Tashma Glymph, Jill Robinson, Brandy Thompson Fisher, Beverly Benson, Idana Bonsi Folson, Minnie Cooper, Beth Lancaster, Rev. Audrey Hailstock, Naa-Lamley Wilson-Aikins, Dr. Dawn Bingham, Beth Neidenbach, Esmaralda Ford Crittenden, Adwoa Serwaa Nuamah, Naa Akuyea Shika Pappoe, Meimuna Bamba, Emefa Kattah, Donna Lancaster, Chioma Asare, Misti Hudson, Naadede Badger, Anne Sakyi, Caroline Brower Goodman, Carmela Antonelli Henderson, Marie Griffin, Letitia DeGraft Okyere, Dr. Mercy Luguterah, Dr. Safoa Addo, Cassie Lloyd, Marva Mcclain, Angela Lyles Butler, Sylvia Brock-Sharpe, Christine Scott, Tessa Kizito, Daniel Nuer, Clemencia Tetteh, Nancy Paschall, Lucia Fields Meeks, Dr. Eliza Osae Kwapong, Naa Kai, Kim Atchley, Page Pettyjohn Birney, Eliza Howell Hyde, Lekesa P Whitner, Rita Mims, Vera Delle Brown, and Jane Ohenewa Gyekye.

My deepest thanks go to every person who generously shared their stories, wisdom, and personal practices. Your thoughtful comments provided the heart and soul of this collection, and I am humbled by your willingness to be so open.

I'm grateful for the AI-assisted research that helped complement and strengthen my writing.

I am also profoundly grateful to the friends, family, and early readers who offered unwavering encouragement and insightful feedback. Your support gave me the strength to see this project through, and your belief in its message helped shape the manuscript into what it is today.

To everyone who contributed, thank you for your honesty and courage. Speaking about sadness is not easy, but in sharing our experiences, we create a space for connection and plant the seeds of hope for one another. This book is a testament to that collective strength. The wisdom shared in these pages comes not from experts, but from real individuals who have navigated their own paths through difficult times. Their experiences serve as a powerful testament to how small, conscious actions can ignite hope and lead to lasting transformation.

If you found value in the book's message, please consider sharing it with a friend who might benefit as well. While the future remains uncertain, let's continue supporting each other.

Together, we can go far.

Marjy Marj

ABOUT THE AUTHOR

Marjy Marj, a Ghanaian American writer based in South Carolina, is known for her inspiring and thought-provoking works. Her 16th book - *Overcoming Sadness* began with a simple question posted on Facebook.

To learn more about her and explore her work, visit www.marjymarj.com.

www.ingramcontent.com/pod-product-compliance
Lightning Source LLC
Chambersburg PA
CBHW060833110426

R18122100002BA/R181221PG42736CBX00041BA/3

*9 7 8 1 9 6 2 5 8 9 2 3 9 *